Implementing Reflective Practice in the K–12 Classroom

This resource offers teachers a simple framework to seamlessly add reflective practice to their day and encourages educators to critically reflect on instructional planning and practice. Commonly used in other busy professions, the *SOAP Notes* structure makes it easy to reflect on student progress through any lesson or learning activity, regardless of grade band or content area. Each category—Subjective, Observation, Assessment, and Planning—allows for documentation of obstacles, difficulties, or challenges within a lesson so educators can address these concerns in subsequent lessons. Each chapter features an in-service teacher who used *SOAP Notes* reflections in their classrooms to improve their instruction and student learning. Contributors are from diverse teaching backgrounds, schools, and student populations. The authors include instructions for using the template in a variety of scenarios, blank worksheets, completed SOAP examples, and important take-aways. Whether there is an hour or only minutes in the day to focus on reflective practice, these teachers demonstrate how this framework makes this activity possible in any classroom. Ideal for preservice and in-service teachers, administrators, and other education professionals across K–12 settings, this accessible read demonstrates the ease of reflective practice while celebrating teacher voices. This simple structure makes adding reflection and intention to teachers' routine immediately doable.

Joanna C. Weaver is an Associate Professor in the School of Inclusive Teacher Education. She is the Adolescence to Young Adult Integrated Language Arts Program Coordinator at Bowling Green State University, USA.

Cynthia D. Bertelsen is an Associate Professor Emeritus at Bowling Green State University, USA.

T0383607

Other Eye on Education Books Available from Routledge
(www.routledge.com/eyeoneducation)

What Do Great Teachers Say? Language All Teachers Can Use to Transform Student Behavior, Parent Relationships, and Classroom Culture
Hal Holloman and Peggy H. Yates (April 2)

The Participatory Creativity Guide for Educators
Edward P. Clapp and Julie Rains (Mar 14)

Cultivating Behavioral Change in K–12 Students: Team-Based Intervention and Support Strategies
Marty Huitt and Gail Tolbert (Feb 9)

The Meditation and Mindfulness Edge: Becoming a Sharper, Healthier, and Happier Teacher
Lisa M. Klein

Embracing Adult SEL: An Educator's Guide to Personal Social Emotional Learning Success
Wendy Turner

Lessons That Last: 185 Reflections on the Life-Shaping Power of a Teacher
Julia Schmidt Hasson and Laura Estes-Swilley

Teach from Your Best Self: A Teacher's Guide to Thriving in the Classroom
Jay Schroder

Pause, Ponder, and Persist in the Classroom: How Teachers Turn Challenges into Opportunities for Impact
Julia Schmidt Hasson

Implementing Reflective Practice in the K–12 Classroom

How to Easily Structure Teaching and Learning Reflections into Your Day

Edited by Joanna C. Weaver
and Cynthia D. Bertelsen

NEW YORK AND LONDON

Designed cover image: © Getty Images

First published 2025
by Routledge
605 Third Avenue, New York, NY 10158

and by Routledge
4 Park Square, Milton Park, Abingdon, Oxon, OX14 4RN

Routledge is an imprint of the Taylor & Francis Group, an informa business

ISBN: 978-1-032-79254-5 (hbk)
ISBN: 978-1-032-79253-8 (pbk)
ISBN: 978-1-003-49346-4 (ebk)

DOI: 10.4324/9781003493464

Typeset in Palatino
by SPi Technologies India Pvt Ltd (Straive)

Contents

Illustrations

Figures

Tables

Dear Readers

It is our privilege to present you with an overview of our book *How to Easily Structure Teaching and Learning Reflections into Your Day*. Our authors are in-service teachers who care about their craft and are eager to reflect and share about their instructional practice. We hope this book encourages educators to critically reflect on instructional planning and practices. We wanted to give voice to the teachers, so they can contribute to the discussion about reflective practice and the impact of reflection on instructional decisions. We believe our book will transform the intentionality of reflective practice.

We hope this book will inspire educators to engage in the stories of the authors and apply *SOAP Notes* reflective strategy in their classrooms. Based on the chapter authors' narratives, it is clear they benefited from the use of *SOAP Notes* as it positively impacted their instruction and student learning. The *SOAP Notes* template (see Figure 0.1) can be utilized across all grade bands and content areas. Included in this book will be figures of the template, instructions, and completed *SOAP Notes* teachers used in their classes.

Reflective practice has been researched extensively, but the use of *SOAP Notes* in classrooms with in-service teachers has been limited. Previously, we have researched *SOAP Notes* usage with preservice teachers and disseminated our findings in five publications and four conference presentations. Based on our curiosities, our natural next step was to ask in-service teachers to implement the *SOAP Notes* in their own classrooms and ask two questions: How did these teachers apply the use of *SOAP Notes*? And how did recording *SOAP Notes* impact their teaching practices? Please feel free to refer to Table 18.1 that covers the takeaways gleaned from each chapter when searching for reflective topics of interest. We hope you enjoy the experiences that our chapter authors have shared about the impact of reflective practice on their instruction as much as we have.

Sincerely,

Joanna C. Weaver & Cynthia D. Bertelsen

Acknowledgements

We want to extend our gratitude and humble appreciation to our chapter authors. Without them, this book would not have been possible. They are 17 teachers across grade bands and content areas whose teaching experiences span from 1 to 34 years. They volunteered to engage in three weeks of intentional and focused reflective practice using *SOAP Notes*.

With their willingness to take *SOAP Notes*, the chapter authors committed to analyzing their notes and writing a chapter focused on the impact reflective practice had on their instruction and/or student learning. Each teacher selected their unit and content, so no chapter is alike. They also chose who was taking the *SOAP Notes*, even though our assumption was that the teachers were writing them. That wasn't always the case, and that made this project even more fascinating.

We had no idea what to expect from the teachers because we had only used *SOAP Notes* with our preservice teachers at the university, so to provide this opportunity to in-service teachers, we were curious how they would approach the challenge. We totally appreciated that the teachers set time aside to dedicate to this project, and we are incredibly grateful for the time they took to analyze their notes and write about their experiences to benefit other teachers.

Based on the chapters, the teachers approached the use of reflective *SOAP Notes* from various lenses and perspectives. Therefore, we thought before moving into the introduction, it was important to briefly describe the demographics of our teacher authors, who come from all over Ohio. For example, ten authors teach in northwest Ohio, three are from central Ohio, one is from southern Ohio, and one is from eastern Ohio. Also, two of the teachers are from charter schools, one teaches at a career tech school, one is at a diocese, six teachers are from suburban schools while one is from an urban school, and another is from a rural school.

In addition to discussing the demographics of the chapter authors, it's important to know that the teachers fall within three categories of experiences with *SOAP Notes*, education, and relationships to Bowling Green State University. For example, nine teachers are BGSU graduates who practiced *SOAP Notes* reflections in their undergraduate program. They are in their first three years of teaching. Four teachers are BGSU graduates with a Master of Education in Reading with between three to five years of teaching experience, and three authors are teacher partners, working as classroom mentor teachers for our undergraduate preservice teachers and have between 20 and 34 years of teaching experience. We truly believe the chapters in this book will help other teachers understand how *SOAP Notes* can be used in any class, grade, or content area.

Meet the Editors and Contributors

Dr. Joanna C. Weaver is an associate professor at Bowling Green State University, focusing on reflective practice, lesson study, and literacy across the curriculum and teaching continuum. She is serving as the Adolescence to Young Adult Integrated Language Arts Program Coordinator. She serves preservice teachers, in-service teachers, and the community. Through collaboration and reflection, Dr. Weaver helps teachers modify instructional practice to improve professional knowledge and literacy practices and strengthen student learning. Furthermore, she facilitates trainings, workshops, and professional development focused on these areas. She has taught both undergraduate and graduate courses as well as Reading grades K–12 and English language arts grades 6–12.

Dr. Cynthia D. Bertelsen is an associate professor emeritus at Bowling Green State University, where she served as coordinator of the Graduate Reading Program for seven years and director of the Martha Gesling Weber Reading Center for three years. Her research focuses on teacher reflective practice, literacy intervention and assessment, teacher preparation and leadership, and adaptive strategies to enhance the learning of all students. She has taught both undergraduate and graduate literacy courses as well as Special Education K–6 in a public school setting.

I am **Matthew Boggs**. I am an integrated language arts teacher with over 20 years of experience in educational initiatives including MTSS integration, digital curriculum development, one-to-one laptop initiatives, and standards-based education practices. I enjoy developing unique pedagogical strategies for the instruction of reading and writing skills. I also enjoy contributing to the field of education through conference presentations and publications on instructional design models for emerging and practicing educators. I received my bachelor's of science (2003) and master's of teaching and curriculum (2006) from Bowling Green State University where I am currently pursuing my Doctorate of leadership studies.

I am **Lindsay Brooks**. I completed my bachelor of science in pharmaceutical sciences at the University of Toledo and continued directly into my doctor of pharmacy program thereafter, while simultaneously completing my master's in criminal justice at Bowling Green State University in Spring 2024. I have had the opportunity to be a guest lecturer for educational courses at Bowling Green State University and assist in providing education to growing schools in Malawi. My next steps include taking on the role as a preceptor for present-day pharmacy students.

I am **Julianna Cajka**, and I am a fifth-year teacher at Toledo Christian Schools. I currently teach 7th and 8th grade writing, literature, and history. I graduated from Bowling Green State University with a bachelor's degree in education.

I am **Sarah Campbell**. I attended Bowling Green State University for my bachelor's degree in early childhood education, then immediately began my reading endorsement and master of reading programs at BGSU. My second year of teaching, I received my 4th and 5th grade endorsement from Walsh University. I hold a preschool through 3rd grade general education and special education degree. I have been teaching 3rd grade for five years. My first two years in 3rd grade were at a charter school in Toledo, Ohio called L Hollingworth School for the Talented and Gifted. At the charter school, I taught reading, writing, and social studies to 50 students. I shared it with one other 3rd grade teacher who taught math and science. The last three years, I have taught 3rd grade at Toth Elementary in Perrysburg, Ohio. At Toth, I teach all subjects and work with three other 3rd grade teachers in my building.

I am **Myka Chavez-EnYart**, and I teach 10th and 12th grade English language arts and 9th–12th grade resource reading in Riverside, Ohio. I am about to complete my sixth year of teaching. I hold a bachelor of science in adolescent young adult integrated language arts education and a master's of education in reading with a K–12 reading endorsement, both from Bowling Green State University. I am also an Ohio's New Educators Member Ambassador, and I serve on my school's Building Leadership Team.

I am **Gabrielle Day**, and I graduated cum laude from BGSU Education AYA ILA program in 2019 and am working on my masters in education in curriculum and teaching with a certificate in instructional design. I live in Toledo with my husband and three boys. I am passionate about books and striving to evoke a love of literacy early in both my classroom and with my littles at home.

I am **Gabrielle Dendinger**, proud two-time Bowling Green State University alumna, graduating with a bachelor of science in adolescence and young adult integrated language arts education in Spring 2018 and a master of education in reading in Spring 2019. I am previously published in the *Mentoring & Tutoring: Partnership in Learning* academic journal for career-related peer mentoring research and am currently preparing to begin my fourth year of teaching as a middle school reading specialist for Marion City Schools.

I am **Erin Dziak**, and I am going into my third year of teaching at St. Thomas Aquinas School in the Cleveland Metropolitan School District. I am the sole English language arts teacher for grades 6–8. My chapter focuses on my 7th grade class. I have my bachelors of science in education and my masters of education in curriculum and teaching, both from Bowling Green State University. I have contributed to two published articles: "Take pause in the quiet moments: Engaging in reflection to guide instruction" (submitted to *The Reading Teacher)* and "Who are the voices? Reflective conversations within assessment" (Submitted to *The Journal of Education and Human Development*).

I am **Amy Farrar**, and I utilized my bachelor's degree in special education from Bowling Green State University during my first nine years as the head of Perrysburg High School's special education program. Enthralled with English after starting inclusion and co-teaching at Perrysburg High School, I obtained my master's in fine arts in English from Bowling Green State University and went on to teach English for 25 years. In my 35th year at Perrysburg High School District, I am currently teaching 11th grade honors American literature and co-teaching 9th grade English. I also researched and co-wrote a college textbook for a master's program on organizational leadership, but most of all in my career, I enjoy discussing the immense importance and efficacy of relational learning.

I am **Jessica Gruesbeck** and I am starting my fifth year of teaching this year. This year, I'm starting brand new at Toledo Public Schools. I graduated from Bowling Green State University with my bachelor's degree in May 2018. I will be teaching 9th and 10th grade English but have also done 11th and 12th.

I am **Emily Hamric**, and I have been teaching for eight years. I am currently in my first year at Allen East High School where I teach Senior ELA, and several communication, literature, and writing CCP courses through both Rhodes State College and BGSU. I hold a bachelors degree in adolescent and young adult integrated language arts education from BGSU, as well as a masters of curriculum and teaching from BGSU. My husband and I live in Lima, Ohio with our two sons.

I am **Dominic Helmstetter** and have taught middle and high school for 15 years. I hold a BA in integrated social studies (Ohio Dominican University), an MA in curriculum and instruction (Heidelberg University), as well as an MEd in education leadership (Lourdes University). I began my teaching career in a diverse high needs community before later serving as Dean of Students and Principal. I later returned to the classroom to teach Junior High social studies before being hired to teach at Perrysburg High School, where I am currently teaching 9th grade government. My instruction focuses on providing hands-on learning experiences centered around promoting engaging and active learning opportunities for students based upon years of graduate level research. In addition to teaching, I enjoy serving on various district wide leadership teams and speaking at educational conferences designed to help boost student engagement and build classroom culture.

I am **Elizabeth Kikel**, and I graduated cum laude from Bowling Green State University with my bachelors in AYA ILA education in 2019. This is my fifth year of teaching with experience at two different schools in Toledo, Woodward High School and Jones Leadership Academy of Business and most recently, at Lutheran High School West in Rocky River, Ohio. I have taught 6th–9th graders within my five years of teaching within the public and private sector. I have been given a variety of opportunities for growth and development over the past five years and am excited to continue learning from each experience.

I am **Grace Mutti** and was born in Strongsville, Ohio. I graduated from Bowling Green State University in 2021 with a bachelor of science in education and is currently in my third year of teaching eighth grade language arts at Port Clinton Middle School. As a teacher, reflective practice and lifelong learning have become instrumental to my teaching and ultimately drove me to pursue a master's degree in curriculum and instruction at Western Governors University. Outside of my language arts classroom and masters classes, I enjoy reading, hiking, and traveling.

I am **Allison Pamer**. After obtaining my bachelor's degree in adolescent young adult education with a specialization in integrated language arts from Bowling Green State University, I taught English language arts at Penta Career Center for four years. At Penta, I had the privilege of teaching ambitious and goal-oriented 10th, 11th, and 12th graders. Now that my husband Matt, dog Beckett, and I are moving to Cleveland, I will be teaching 9th and 10th grade at Lorain County Joint Vocational School. Career-tech education has become a great passion of mine over the years and I'm so grateful to continue doing what I love. I am currently working toward obtaining my masters in educational leadership as I teach and look forward to what the future holds!

I am **Shoupra Shikwana**, and this is my sixth year of teaching. I am currently a seventh grade ELA teacher at Springfield Middle School in Holland, Ohio. I graduated with a bachelor''s degree in Adolescence to Young Adult Integrated Language Arts from Bowling Green State

University in 2018. I also graduated with a MAT degree from Miami University''s Ohio Writing Project in 2022. During my graduate studies, I researched and presented strategies to motivate student writers.

 I am **Anna Wank**. I am a 2018 graduate of Bowling Green State University's bachelor of education program. I currently teach with Findlay City Schools as a high school English teacher with six classes of freshmen! The 2023–2024 school year marks my sixth year as a teacher, and I am continuing my education through Bowling Green State University with a master of arts in English with a specialization in professional writing and rhetoric. I am also taking an active role in her union, participating on local, regional, state, and national levels. I was honored to be one of seven nationally funded representatives from Ohio to attend the NEA Minority Leadership Training and Women's Leadership Training Seminars to Advance Racial & Social Justice, as well as a recipient of the NWOEA's Graduate Scholarship and Promising Leader Award. I continue to read and write extensively in my spare time, as well as bake, craft, and pursue theater. I want to thank my family, partner, mentors, friends, and pets for their love and support!

Introduction

SOAP Notes is a tool that preservice teachers as well as classroom teachers can use to compile the relevant information about their teaching and how students are progressing through the curriculum through lessons and learning activities. They also provide an opportunity for teachers to document particular obstacles, difficulties, or challenges within the lesson so that they can come back and address these types of challenges or obstacles in their subsequent lessons. They certainly improve communication, not only internally as educators are reflecting but also with colleagues. Furthermore, they provide a structure for developing plans to assist teachers as they move through the curriculum to achieve their goals.

The acronym *SOAP* stands for **S**ubjective, **O**bservation, **A**ssessment, and **P**lanning. The *SOAP Notes* promote reflective practices that can strengthen reflective dialogue. They actually started in the medical field to organize records and thinking (Cameron, 2002). Many and Many (2014) applied this framework to the field of education. Building on Many and Many's (2014) work on reflective practice (Schön, 1983), we have helped preservice and in-service teachers record complex situations by encouraging them to organize their thoughts, modify instruction, and engage in communication and reflection by using a modified version of *SOAP Notes* (Mills et al., 2020; Weaver & Mutti, 2021; Weaver et al., 2020, 2021, 2022).

When using the *SOAP Notes* method of reflection, teachers can quickly identify challenges within instruction and determine changes that might improve student learning (Beck & Kosnik, 2001; Kovacs & Corrie, 2017; Mills et al., 2020; Weaver & Mutti, 2021; Weaver et al., 2020, 2021, 2022; Vygotsk, 1978). *SOAP Notes*

DOI: 10.4324/9781003493464-1

provide evidence of data, assessment, and space to record and plan next steps. What you can see in Figure 0.1 are detailed instructions that we give our preservice teachers (PTs) on how to complete their *SOAP Notes*. We provided these instructions to our in-service teachers for this book project.

Evaluation of Instruction (SOAP)	By:		Date:	
S	**Subjective**: students' willingness to participate, demeanor, body language, attitude. Teacher's perceptions and reflections			
O	**Observation** of student learning: anecdotal notes			
A	**Assessing** student learning: Progress monitoring, running records, oral or written comprehension			
P	**Planning** for next lesson: use bullet points			
Challenges: What challenges did you encounter while working with your students?				
Further Learning: What else do you need to know how to do?				

FIGURE 0.1 *SOAP Notes* template.

Source: Weaver, J. C., Hartzog, M., Murnen, T., & Bertelsen, C. D. (2019). Bowling Green State University

We noticed a couple areas that needed further development when observing PTs' reflective practice. We added two more categories, *Challenges* and *Further Learning*. Because we are trying to encourage our students not to just reflect on how things went and what needs to happen next, we really wanted them to think more deeply. Therefore, the *Challenges and Further Learning* sections addressed the critical thinking and reflection we wanted them to experience.

SOAP Notes help teachers center themselves and focus on student learning and the impact of instruction (Mills et al., 2020; Weaver & Mutti, 2021; Weaver et al., 2020, 2021, 2022). There are a lot of different ways we can use *SOAP Notes* within the classroom, and in this book, we are focusing on 17 teachers' approaches to their use of *SOAP Notes* and reflective practice and how it impacted their instructional decision-making.

Chapter Summaries

Section one of the book focuses on professional learning and the connections between the medical use of *SOAP Notes* and the educational use of *SOAP Notes*. In Chapter 1, Lindsay, a graduate student in pharmacy, focuses on the current use of medical *SOAP Notes* in her graduate courses. We included her chapter because *SOAP Notes* began in the medical field (Cameron, 2002) and transitioned into the education field (Many & Many, 2014). We thought it was fascinating to see the similarity as Lindsay described her training and experience as she practiced using *SOAP Notes* and how these experiences truly paralleled our undergraduate preservice teachers, but also, now, the in-service teachers who told their story here in this book. Lindsay described how her thinking transformed over time as she recorded her observations using *SOAP Notes*. In her chapter, she admitted that she still has a lot to learn but sees the benefits and changes in the way she processes, collects, and records information that is shared with other medical professionals.

As Dominic analyzed *SOAP Notes* and discovered the alignment from the medical *SOAP Notes* to educational *SOAP Notes*, in Chapter 2, he tells the story of his sister who is a nurse and used *SOAP Notes* to inform her practice. He compares the similarities of outcomes between what his sister told him about her *SOAP Notes* and what he experienced using reflective practice in the classroom. Dominic focuses on the impact *SOAP Notes* had on his day-to-day instructional practices. He made changes from class to class and across the week of instruction. He was able to use *SOAP Notes* as a tool to better meet his students' learning needs, and he worked hard to personalize learning opportunities and incorporate experiential learning and project-based learning activities.

Another example of this transformation of thinking is in Chapter 3. Matt discusses how *SOAP Notes* shaped his pedagogical choices and instructional strategies used in the classroom, but it took him a little time to get used to taking the notes. He describes his transition in thinking and how he truly began to value the use of intentional reflective practice. Furthermore, he discusses how using *SOAP Notes* informed his instructional practice and the selection of strategies that would further engage his students.

In Chapters 4–8, teachers continue to discuss how *SOAP Notes* impacted their instructional practice. Chapters 4 through 6 specifically focus on student choice and engagement; while Chapters 7 and 8 immerse readers in the experience of two teachers who discuss the application of *SOAP Notes*. Allison's Chapter 4 focuses on scaffolding and creating lessons that created new opportunities for student choice through project and inquiry learning. She goes into more depth about student reactions to learning prompts and content. She discusses more fully the methods and techniques she implemented to ensure student success. She writes that reflective teaching practices are integral to a teacher's journey of growth. She discusses that a simple, effective, and tangible way to monitor reflective teaching is through *SOAP Notes*. She explains how *SOAP Notes* provided her the opportunity to really identify how students interacted with the lesson, and what she can do to revise the lesson to strengthen it the next time.

Similar to Chapter 4, Gabrielle unpacks how her teaching improved and was strengthened by using *SOAP Notes* in Chapter 5. She focuses on how to hold students accountable for independent reading and emphasizes student engagement and selection of reading materials. Furthermore, she emphasizes co-teaching strategies as well as challenges with group work and how she had to move back and forth with online teaching. She draws us into her story, telling us about her students drifting off into space and how she had to modify her plans to fully engage her students. In addition, she explains how *SOAP Notes* helped her think about accommodating student learning needs more efficiently as well as strengthen her own instruction and how they inspired her to make some other reflections on additional work she wanted to do as an educator.

In Chapter 6, Emily is very honest with her analysis of the impact of *SOAP Notes*. She discusses how the framework is different from other reflective practices. The *SOAP Notes* model forced her to focus her attention to her students' demeanor, body language, and attitudes throughout class, specifically in the Subjective section of the *SOAP Notes*. Her voice is palpable as she discusses the power of writing down these observations in the notes and what she learned from seeing her observations in print. Not only is her own voice palpable but also she discovered the power of student voice. The instruction she chose to abandon to focus on student learning and choice surprised her, and she gave credit to the use of the intentional reflective practice of *SOAP Notes*. Finally, she shares that *SOAP Notes* allowed her to look at the "human" side of her job rather than just the pedagogical, instructional side.

In Chapter 7, Myka looks at reflection as a way to stretch her thinking about teaching, learning, and student engagement. She discusses how much pressure is on teachers, and doing this chapter project was something she was not too excited about, but upon engagement in reflective practice, she realized it improved the trust between her students and her. Part of that was because while using *SOAP Notes*, she began having more confidence in her lesson delivery. Through close reflection, she was able to build upon and modify her plans to meet the learning and engagement needs of her students. Because of what she read in her *SOAP Notes* reflections, she flipped her mindset and put the responsibility of learning on her students instead of just on herself. *SOAP Notes* reflections provided the opportunity she needed to empower herself and empower her students in their learning and realized that she had to intentionally make the choice to reflect each day to see a difference in her teaching and learning.

Like Myka, Anna describes in Chapter 8 how *SOAP Notes* helped her critically think about her students' learning. Anna realized that *SOAP Notes* benefitted her because she was able to address the learning abilities and capabilities of her students who were identified as gifted. She discussed the impact *SOAP Notes* had on her thinking around grouping to maximize student interaction and learning, student investment, and creativity. She designed learning tasks that encouraged creativity and innovation. After completing her notes, she found herself asking more questions about student interests and effective engagement. She saw her thinking transform into a more student-centered approach to teaching and learning, establishing rapport by creating a warm and welcoming environment that promotes motivation and growth-mindset.

Both authors of Chapter 9 and 10 specifically take a deep dive into their instruction and learning using *SOAP Notes*. Chapter 9 demonstrates Erin's vulnerability. She expresses that teaching has been hard the last couple years, and she is honest about these teaching challenges. She reveals that taking *SOAP Notes* helped her see trends in her writings and problems in her classroom that needed to be addressed. She walks us through her experiences, and they were powerful, relatable, and discussions that will be meaningful to teachers.

Gabrielle writes in Chapter 10 about her powerful journey in constructing a unit based on student choice. She had experiences using *SOAP Notes* at the university, so Gabby knew the power of written reflection. She realized that she would critically benefit from writing *SOAP Notes* in her class. It would help her view her own daily reflections and assess her units as she adjusted and made modifications. Gabby walks us through her day-to-day *SOAP Notes* to highlight her thinking as she approached her daily instruction and what needed to be changed along the way.

Chapters 11 through 13 focus on reinforcing student–teacher relationships. In Chapter 11, Amy uses *SOAP Notes* in a way that reinforced these relationships. The chapter is unique because *SOAP Notes* were used differently than the other chapter authors. Amy's students evaluated her teaching with *SOAP Notes* versus Amy taking the reflective notes. She asked students to give her feedback using the *SOAP Notes* to reflect on her teaching. Amy was encouraged using *SOAP Notes* because she was able to observe a specific aspect of instructional dynamics. For example, she observed students' different nonverbal cues. Amy shares that having students participating in the *SOAP Notes* process confounded and challenged her, and that created her greatest growth because she had to act on what she needed to know as an educator.

Chapter 12 is written by Sarah, who is the only early childhood teacher who submitted a chapter to our book. Her chapter provides a different but parallel perspective to those teaching in grades 7–12. Sarah provided three themes in her chapter, including statewide testing and the Third Grade Guarantee, challenges of looking closely at informational text, and the writing process. She states that recording and analyzing *SOAP Notes* helped her continue to improve herself as an educator as she focused on helping students make text connections and additional strategies on test taking that could be used in multiple learning environments.

Chapter 13 focuses on Grace's *SOAP Notes*. Grace was a first-year teacher who had taken *SOAP Notes* during methods and student teaching at the university. Using *SOAP Notes*, she was able to learn a lot about her students' strengths, weaknesses, and interests as well as her own instructional strengths and weaknesses. For example, pacing was a challenge for her. This was clearly revealed in her analysis of *SOAP Notes*, and she had to overcome this challenge and used *SOAP Notes* as a place to record her growth each day as she modified her instructional plans. She learned the most from her on-the-spot teaching and immediate adjustments. She also found that reflection helped her think across the unit versus just her day-to-day teaching.

Chapters 14–17 primarily focus on student needs that were highlighted within the teachers' experiences using *SOAP Notes*. Lizzi writes in Chapter 14 that the largest factors she noticed from her notes were students' competence levels, formative assessments, behavior management, and interactive activities. Lizzi shows she is incredibly forward-thinking and believes in the power of reflection through *SOAP Notes*. She believes it helped her find students' passions, success, and a love of learning because she was able to focus and reflect on them and how her instruction and decision-making impacts their learning.

Chapter 15, written by Julianna, provides a practical look at the benefits and limitations of *SOAP Notes*. Julianna carefully laid out her insights of reflective practice, highlighting the strengths and benefits of *SOAP Notes*. She stated that in her experience, reflection helped her to be more aware of her students' emotional responses to the content, found ways to manage their frustration, and gave them opportunities to shine. She also noted a couple limitations such as that reflections must be taken seriously and not just become quick explanations without carefully analyzing situations.

In Chapter 16, Jessica focuses on student responses and behavior, specifically emphasizing the subjective section of the *SOAP Notes*. She wanted to explore more student-directed learning, engagement, and motivation. She discovered from her use of *SOAP Notes* that reflective practice is one of the most important parts of being a teacher and that she had to be able to look back at what she taught and think about how she taught it and decide if it went well or if she needed to change her delivery. Jessica realized through the consistent use of *SOAP Notes* that she needed to continue reflecting and modifying instruction so her students could succeed.

Chapter 17 is the perfect ending to the *SOAP Notes* story. Shoupra shares her experiences during a difficult year. She discussed how teaching is a puzzle and the pieces come together to form a picture. While teachers are amid the teaching puzzle, watching all the pieces come together, Shoupra asked if teachers should use the masterpiece as a roadmap for next year or crumble it to begin again? In addition, she shared strategies she used to improve her classroom management and instruction, and she also tried to discover incentives to motivate her students. She used *SOAP Notes* to reflect on the strategies and ideas used in her class, and follow-up questions she had. She realized after analyzing her notes that her overall objective was to create small and achievable goals for her students to work toward together, thus creating a positive learning environment for everybody in the room.

Chapter 18 draws together the take-aways of the chapter authors after they used *SOAP Notes* to reflect on their instruction and student learning. What we found most interesting as we read the chapters in this book was how *SOAP Notes* helped with individual thinking and reflection and served as a catalyst for conversations. Medical *SOAP Notes* guided the implementation of educational *SOAP Notes* and opened new pathways for reflective practice. This book highlighted ways educators can organize their data, establish goals, and document next steps. In general, the authors of these chapters felt confident using the *SOAP Notes*, and every author noted instructional benefits.

References

Beck, C., & Kosnik, C. (2001). Reflection-in-action: In defense of thoughtful teaching. *Curriculum Inquiry*, *31*(2), 217–227. https://doi.org/10.1111/0362-6784.00193

Cameron, S. (2002). Learning to write case notes using the SOAP format. *Journal of Counseling & Development*, *80*, 286–292.

Kovacs, L., & Corrie, S. (2017). Building reflective capability to enhance coaching practice. *The Coaching Psychologist*, *13*(1), 4–12.

Many, T. W., & Many, B. T. (2014). Best practices. *TEPSA News*, *2*(2). www.tepsa.org

Mills, A. M., Weaver, J. C., Bertelsen, C. D., & Dziak, E. T. (2020). Take pause in quiet moments: Engaging in reflection to guide instruction. *Reading Teacher*, *74*(1), 71–78.

Schön, D. (1983). *The reflective practitioner: How professionals think in action*. London, UK: Temple Smith.

Vygotsky, L. S. (1978). *Mind in society: The development of higher psychological processes*. Harvard University Press.

Weaver, J. C., Murnen, T., Hartzog, M., & Bertelsen, C. D. (2020). Reaching incarcerated youth for literacy: The collaborative evolution of the MILE program. In *Literacy across the community: A handbook of research and praxis*. Routledge, Taylor & Francis Group.

Weaver, J. C., Bertelsen, C. D., & Othman, K. (2022). SOAP notes promotes habits of reflective practice. *Journal on Empowering Teaching Excellence* (in press).

Weaver, J. C., & Mutti, G. (2021). A study of incarcerated youth: The effect of interest on reading comprehension and engagement? *Journal on Empowering Teaching Excellence*, *5*(2), 46–67. https://digitalcommons.usu.edu/jete/vol5/iss2/6

Weaver, J. C., Bertelsen, C. D., Murnen, T., & Glanz, J. (2021). Through the eyes of the mentor: Understanding the adolescent developing readers. *Journal on Empowering Teaching Excellence*, *5*(1), 28–47.

Part I

Professional Learning

Connections between Medical and Educational SOAP Notes

1

SOAP Notes' Impact in Pharmacy School

Lindsay Brooks

GETTING TO KNOW THE AUTHOR

♦ Final-year Pharm.D. graduate student
♦ Use of medical *SOAP Notes* in graduate school
♦ Application of medical *SOAP Notes* during rotations in community pharmacy and hospitals

---

From a medical perspective, *SOAP Notes* are used to establish subjective and objective assessments and plans to explain the results of patients' visits in a systematic manner. *SOAP Notes* are an established strategy that is modeled and practiced in medical, nursing, and pharmacy schools to help undergraduate and graduate students learn to record all patients' data using subjective and objective problem lists and statements, solution and goals, counseling points, and main points of communication with patients. In addition, *SOAP Notes* help record and measure the effectiveness of treatments and further aid in the modifying of

DOI: 10.4324/9781003493464-3

treatment plans as needed. They document data for other medical professionals to be able to quickly and easily access as well as understand patient records. With all *SOAP Notes* following a consistent format, professionals know exactly where to look for the patient data they are attempting to access. *SOAP Notes* may be shared among medical professionals who request advice from other providers and medical personnel.

Students in the medical field use *SOAP Notes* to accurately organize data in a legible manner that makes the patient's history and current problems easier to understand because they only contain pertinent information. While in school, students are presented cases to convey practical information in a clinical case setting. The goal of this is to teach students to summarize and describe the medical story of patients accurately in transition of care settings.

S: Subjective

Subjective information is descriptive in nature. This data is obtained by listening to the patient or patient's family members as they describe their symptoms and current problems, as well as their history. The subjective section of the *SOAP Notes* includes the chief complaint, history of present illness, past medical history, social history, family history, review of systems, allergies, and medications that are obtained in the patient interview such as over-the-counter medications (see Table 1.1).

TABLE 1.1 Medical *SOAP Notes*: Subjective

Chief Complaint (CC)
◆ Reason for a visit as stated by the patient, may be written as a quote or a general reason ◆ May include symptoms and/or complaints ◆ Is short in length: one to two full sentences or short phrases ◆ Recommended that you use patient initials, age, and sex in the first line to orient the reader to the patient's information

(Continued)

TABLE 1.1 (Continued)

History of Present Illness (HPI)   ◆ Chronological and accurate depiction of patient's history related only to the patient's chief complaint   ◆ Relays information that was collected during the patient interview
Past Medical History (HPI)   ◆ Listing of all current and past medical diagnoses, surgeries, and procedures   ◆ Include the duration of these disease states as well as dates
Social History (SH)   ◆ Current and past use and quantity of tobacco, alcohol, and illicit drugs   ◆ Lifestyle habits of diet and exercise   ◆ Psychosocial factors including but not limited to education, living situation, occupation, marital status, religious beliefs, financial situation, language spoken, and so forth as needed when it is pertinent to the patient's chief complaint
Family History (FH)   ◆ Major medical conditions of first-degree relatives, their ages, and causes of death if applicable
Review of Systems (ROS)   ◆ Series of questions that get answered focused on a head-to-toe review of the patient's body   ◆ This may be related to symptoms that are described by the patient
Allergies   ◆ Drug name, dose (if applicable), reaction the patient had, and treatment (if known)   ◆ If none, NKDA (no known drug allergies) should be documented in this section   ◆ This section should not be left blank
Medication History   ◆ The list of all current list of medications collected during the patient interview, including prescription, over the counter, vitamins and supplements, and vaccinations (name, route, and date)   ◆ The name, strength, route, frequency and directions, as well as start and stop dates of the medications   ◆ Information about patient adherence   ◆ Adverse effects that the patient is experiencing

TABLE 1.2 Medical *SOAP Notes*: Objective

Vital Signs
◆ Blood pressure, heart rate, respiratory rate, temperature, height, weight
Calculated Data
◆ Age, body mass index, ideal body weight, creatinine clearance (calculated based on the Cockcroft-Gault equation)
Medication Profile
◆ The list of all current medications collected or verified by a pharmacy system, including prescription, over the counter, vitamins and supplements, vaccinations (name, route, and date)
◆ The name, strength, route, frequency, and directions, as well as start and stop dates of the medications
◆ Adverse effects that the patient is experiencing

O: Objective

Objective information is measured in a direct manner, based on physically examining the patient, listening to breathing sounds and heart beats, visual appearances, and laboratory testing. The objective section of the *SOAP Notes* includes laboratory tests, diagnostic tests and procedures, vital signs, physical assessments, calculated data, medication history obtained or verified by a pharmacy, and calculated data (see Table 1.2).

A: Assessment

Assessment statements are used to identify and prioritize the patient's reason for visiting the office. The patient's medical history is assessed and compared with problems that are occurring and whether they are medically related. Their history could possibly interfere with optimal therapeutic outcomes as well as assessments of patients' potential health risks and preventative care treatments. Assessment statements should be summarized in a manner that describes the problem secondary to the cause as evidenced by the subjective and objective evidence provided. No new information should be presented in this statement. The goal of assessment statements is to state the problem, the status of the condition (whether it is controlled or uncontrolled, newly diagnosed, mild, moderate, severe, etc.), information pertinent to the problem, potential risk factors, any drugs the patient is currently on to treat this problem, and the goals of treatment.

P: Plan

The plan is designed to state what the medical professionals are hoping to accomplish and how they will educate the patient while in the office for a visit. This statement includes a recommendation of non-drug therapies, drug therapies, monitoring for patient safety and efficacy, as well as what is necessary to communicate to the patient and caregivers about possible reactions that may occur, drug interactions, how to correctly administer the drug, and possible referrals to other providers. Furthermore, within the plan, a follow-up time is established and should include the date and time a patient should be seen, as well as the prognosis of their symptoms and when they may begin to resolve. In addition, at this follow-up appointment, additional evaluations occur, including whether the patient should continue this therapy or if any changes in treatments are required.

As students progress into their professional years, *SOAP Notes* shift in terms of what they include. Semester one was our introduction to *SOAP Notes*. We were introduced to finding the problem within a case a patient was experiencing, and we recorded the possible solutions in the *SOAP Notes* format described previously. Initially, we would always identify the three most pertinent problems within our given cases, and we would include all data that pertained to the patient. For example, we would list all medications that the patient was on without considering the chief complaint of the patient. When presenting the problem using the *SOAP Notes* template, it was displayed in one sentence that followed the "problem—secondary to—as evidenced by" format.

While recording *SOAP Notes*, we focused on extracting the most important details in cases. For example, instead of listing each of the medications the patient was on, we would only list the medications for the patient that pertained to their chief complaint. For example, if a patient was experiencing an asthma exacerbation, we would only list the medications that the patient was on to help with their asthma and anything that they had tried to help with the exacerbation or medications that the doctor and/or hospital gave the patient to treat this exacerbation. Completing the *SOAP Notes* helps us differentiate between the major and minor data that relate to the patient's chief complaint.

Utilizing *SOAP Notes* has shifted my thinking. As my knowledge within the medical field grows, so do the complexities of the cases that I must solve; however, because *SOAP Notes* have been scaffolded across the semesters, the *SOAP Notes* have gradually become more comprehensible, and producing them has become more efficient.

SOAP Notes have overall really altered the manner in which I process, collect, and record information. My thinking has significantly changed because of using *SOAP Notes*. They have really helped me by changing the way that I intake data from a difficult case and simplify it into a brief and concise document that is easily read by others.

TAKE-AWAYS

SOAP Notes **reflective practice helped:**

♦ Accurately organize patient records
♦ Provide knowledge of patient history
♦ Establish goals
♦ Serve as efficient, comprehensive conversation starters and communication with medical professionals

2

Reflection in Education

Dominic Helmstetter

GETTING TO KNOW THE AUTHOR

- ♦ 9th grade government teacher
- ♦ 15th year of teaching
- ♦ Suburban high school

In the words of John Dewey, "We do not learn from experience, we learn from reflecting on experience" (1933, p. 78). As a teacher, I am constantly reflecting on the way material is received and how my students are interpreting the information we study. I recently came across a study on reflective practice in the field of nursing. "Reflection" and "nursing" aren't words typically used simultaneously, but my little sister is a nurse. My perception of her work has always been along the lines of life and death, not reflection. In her work, she follows protocols she must adhere to when visiting patients, and her decision-making has a significant impact on the health of those patients.

I recently asked my sister about reflection and the impact it has on her profession, and she said that reflection allows nurses to adjust style and strategy and improve their skills during each

DOI: 10.4324/9781003493464-4

shift. It also allows her to improve communication with her coworkers and patients. I never really stopped to consider that reflection impacts her work as reflection has impacted my work. Bullman and Schutz (2013) state, "We believe that reflection is essential for effective and person-centered professional practice" (p. 1).

When I hear my sister reference words such as "adjust," "strategize," and "improve," it helps me realize that we are both (teacher and nurse) reflecting in the same way to help us grow and expand our abilities to be effective in our professions. We are both using these experiences to reflect on how effective we are while working with other people.

So how does reflection impact teachers in education? What is reflection for educators? How am I adjusting my practice to improve so I am effectively meeting their needs? When I sit back and consider these questions, I know from my years of learning that there is some literature that can tell me about reflection. Dewey (1933) states that an experience is an interaction between the individual and the environment. When thinking about experiences, I immediately reflect back to my classroom and each of my students. Reflective practice helps impact the way I approach teaching and learning.

Since reflection is active, teachers must examine beliefs, assumptions, and implications (Dewey, 1933). Reflection on experiences and current teaching practices can help us accumulate more understanding and challenge beliefs while actively considering other possibilities. It's true that challenging ourselves in this way can create discomfort. However, this discomfort could also lead us to new and exciting responses and ideas that could have a far greater impact on the learning of our students.

Kolb's (1984) theory of experiential learning outlines the process whereby adults can learn from their experiences. Kolb's learning cycle helps perpetuate learning through reflection. This learning experience moves along a cyclical path for further learning, action, and more reflection. This philosophy asks us to take our experiences and review the quality of those interactions. It challenges us to take a long look at the (learning) outcomes of those experiences and shift when needed. Like my sister says, we need to shift and strategize our next steps, so we can ensure that we are maximizing the (learning) outcomes for our students. Dewey (1933) and Kolb (1984) both include reflection in their theories. Dewey emphasizes constant and active reflection of experiences, while Kolb views reflection in a cyclical manner that emphasizes a more defined focus on the impact to learning. In both cases, the intention is to review your practices regularly so you can further shift your instruction. In another study, Schön (1983) describes the capacity to consciously think about what we are doing while we are doing it. Schön recognizes the importance of reflecting back "in order to discover how our knowing-in-action may have contributed to an unexpected outcome" (para. 21).

At the heart of these theories is the act of reflection. How we learn and grow from reflective practice may be different for each teacher, but the goal of improvement must always be embedded in the results of those reflections. The ability to change and amend your practice is essential to instructional improvement and student learning. For example, I've experimented with audio and video recordings of my teaching during the school day. After reviewing and reflecting on the additional information that I was able to collect, I was able to impact my teaching by adjusting the way that I question students about content and the way I stand and walk around the classroom, and I was also able to adjust the way I present and clarify information, all because of these reflective exercises. The key in these reflections was using and collecting ongoing evidence and making meaningful improvements based on that evidence. Developing better questioning techniques centered around depth of knowledge is an evidence-based outcome that I was able to emphasize in my classroom because of my reflection.

In this chapter, my goals were to reflect on my classroom experiences through *SOAP Notes* while studying the impact or outcomes that these learning practices are having on my students' learning. Furthermore, I wanted to examine the impact these reflective notes had on my day-to-day instructional practices. Why did students understand or not understand? What informed those decisions? and Was there growth? are all questions I've considered throughout this process.

There were 24 total students in my class. I used *SOAP Notes* from the same class spanning across the second quarter. Various holiday breaks and exams interrupted the overall flow of my note taking but should still provide a clear view of the impact reflection has had in my classroom. The content changed throughout the time period. The following patterns emerged when reflecting on the 15-day period of collecting *SOAP Notes*.

Figure 2.1 describes the immediate impact of reflection. I looked at changes made to the subsequent class of students, the following day with the same students, and the next instructional lesson with the same students. During the 15 days of *SOAP Notes*, I made immediate changes prior to the next class of students 60% of the time. The change often occurred during the lesson or after the lesson. Direct changes for the following school day were minimal—2% of the time. Although limited, based upon student understanding, reteaching or additional remediation was required to ensure the material was fully grasped. I realized I needed to add a greater challenge for students prior to teaching it again. This occurred 40% of the time. In these cases, new or additional information was often added to better connect with the previous day's learning.

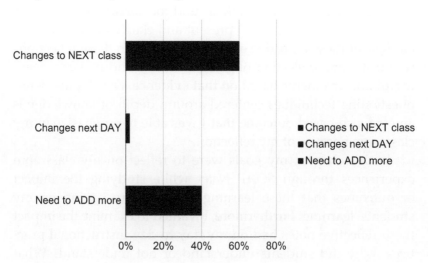

FIGURE 2.1 Immediate impact of reflection

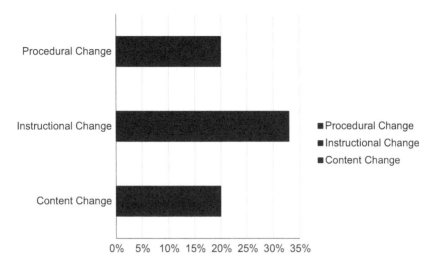

FIGURE 2.2 Changes as a result of reflection

Figure 2.2 describes the type of changes that were needed as a result of the reflections. Procedural adjustments such as timing, better execution, or improved transitioning were necessary 20% of the time. Changes in instructional techniques such as the tools being used (paper or technology) or the style of organizational charting (3×3 chart, T Chart) to help organize the material more effectively for students had to be revisited 30% of the time. I also noticed that modifications were required that included adding new content material to further extend learning or better clarify something in the lesson 20% of the time.

By the end of the first semester, my classes were averaging 90–94% on each of their tests. Consistent monitoring and reflection were a large part of achieving continued improvement, but giving students the chance to also reflect and set goals for continued improvement (while identifying areas where they struggled) was equally as important during this process.

Now let's take a deeper look into some of these lessons. The first area of reflection was focused on lessons involving the judicial branch. During this unit, students started by engaging in a "Judicial Escape Room" activity. The purpose of this activity was to expose students to key names and details in the judicial branch. Students were given hypernotes to dig deeper into the material they were initially exposed to during the escape room. During this particular lesson, there were some technological complications that needed to be fixed prior to the next class.

Student feedback was extremely helpful in understanding why certain functions in the Google form were not working as I intended. In addition, reflecting on student questions and comments allowed me to add more detail and better digital feedback prior to my next class. This allowed students to receive improved, timely virtual feedback and allowed me to be more strategic in targeting and supporting struggling students during this lesson. Finally, the experience with my first class allowed me to preemptively give additional tips and hints on how to best organize time and complete the tasks correctly and effectively going into my later classes. Reflecting on this lesson, improved virtual and individualized feedback was a major benefit of *SOAP* noting.

As a result of the efforts during the first lesson, the second day of learning was shifted and changed in order to meet the interests and levels of the students. For example, a new sorting activity was added to the lesson that included details about the judicial branch such as names, numbers, and job responsibilities. The sorting activity allowed students to take material that they completed last class and extend it further by connecting it with what they know but also included questions that allowed them to extend it into new areas.

Many instructional changes (i.e., sorting activity and video extension) were a direct result of the reflection and conversation with students yesterday. For example, we watched a video interview of two judges (Ginsburg and Breyer) to compare and contrast the legal opinions and views of each. This further allowed me to model notes on the videos but also added a real-world view on the details they sorted earlier. Next to the video screen, there were guided notes with questions. Then on the white board, I took my own notes where answers could be found simultaneously while watching the video clips.

In the next class, the goal was to review current events and connect it to our material while researching and preparing to present various court cases. What actually happened was that students were interested and asked many questions about the current events (e.g., the situation in Ukraine). While reflecting during and after the lesson, I realized I needed additional resources to help paint a larger picture of the events unfolding in Ukraine and the U.S. response to those growing tensions. This also gave students a chance to see how past material is being used on a daily basis throughout the government. For example, we reviewed a letter from Congress reminding the president of his war limitations, which allowed us to see the balance of power and checks that exist in the constitution.

An immediate change that occurred from one class to the next was to create a larger focus on the current events and outline the connections to our material instead of rushing through it to get to another new piece of information. After spending time expanding the focus on our government and how it manages current issues in the world, students were given some additional in class time to review and prepare for the hypernotes activity we were planning to work on during our next session. The extra time on current events and the added bonus of previewing material prior to digging into it deeper were extremely beneficial. Students walked into class more confident the next day knowing what they would be getting into.

SOAP Notes allowed for more student voice and choice. Specifically, there were several moments when using current events and following student questions led to more meaningful learning opportunities and more meaningful learning outcomes. Using local history and current events is something that I need to purposefully build in more for each lesson. Looking for more local examples can help students connect more with their world.

When looking back at the entire experience, I am really happy that I was able to reflect and consider the ways we collect and use information throughout the learning cycle. Before this exercise, I naturally reflected and adjusted almost as a routine part of my teaching. In many ways it was a practice I didn't think much about but knew I had to tweak depending on the students and types of class dynamics that I had. When I see that 60% of the time I am changing something prior to the next class, that number jumps out and startles me a little bit. However, when I dig deeper and consider all the little things that are adjusted from class to class, it puts that number into focus and makes me feel like it should be a little higher. After all, my goal is to adjust to each of my learners and provide them with individualized learning experiences that are catered to what they need to best understand the content.

The *SOAP Notes* format forces me to evaluate my teaching from a different angle. Walking into this experience, I knew that I had amazing students. Taking the time to observe student actions, words, responses, facial reactions, class rapport, time management, group collaborations, and overall energy were extremely powerful for me. Reflecting on my notes and seeing how willing, excited, and energetic my students were during our activities was impactful. Additionally, monitoring assessments and intentionally planning for change was the area I found myself looking at the most. Planning to improve and adjust was the most gratifying part of the entire process.

When considering the experience as a whole, it allowed me to see parallels between reflection in education and reflection in other professions, such as the medical field. Initially, I had misconceptions regarding the role of nurses and reflection, but through research and experience, I found it valuable to recognize the elements of action and planning, in any capacity, to help drive positive change and future growth. As discussed earlier, adjusting and strategizing with an eye toward improving is something that all professions can embrace.

TAKE-AWAYS

SOAP Notes **reflective practice helped:**

◆ Elevates student voice
◆ Supports student agency and choice
◆ Teachers adapt teaching practices
◆ Teachers revise instructional strategies
◆ Provides more time for teacher mentoring and guiding of student learning
◆ Instructional decision-making

References

Bullman, C., & Schutz, S. (2013). *Reflective practice in nursing* (5th ed.). Wiley and Sons.

Dewey, J. (1933). *How we think: A restatement of reflective thinking to the educative process*. D.C. Heath.

Kolb, D. A. (1984). *Experiential learning: Experience as a source of learning and development*. Prentice-Hall.

Schön, D. (1983). *Getting started with reflective practice*. Cambridge Assessment International Education. https://www.cambridge-community.org.uk/professional-development/gswrp/index.html

3

SOAP Notes

Supports Reflective Practice and Aligns with OTES 2.0

Matthew Boggs

GETTING TO KNOW THE AUTHOR

- 9th grade English teacher
- 19th year of teaching
- Suburban high school

When considering the influential experiences that shape peda-gogical choices and instructional strategies used in the class-room, reflective practice is becoming a valued approach. Like many teachers at the start of their career, I recalled utilizing handwritten notes on lessons, daily lesson logs where I included successes and failures, compiled printed materials for units as they were developed, and made revisions from year to year. Over the course of my first five to six years as an educator, I had subconsciously applied reflective practice to several aspects of my teaching pedagogy.

DOI: 10.4324/9781003493464-5

At that time, I was not realizing the value of reflective practice and how it began to shape my teaching career. Specific areas that greatly benefited my teaching impacted student success. My progression of reflective practice became a record of my pedagogical evolution, and this is when the *SOAP Notes* reflective strategy was introduced to me. An interesting attribute of *SOAP Notes* is that it encompasses several areas connected to both student and instructor growth in a simple, guided approach. When considering the overwhelming task of what it means to be an educator, *SOAP Notes* is a simple framework in which educators can focus on observing success and failures while logging objectives, expectations, and relevant questions that teachers should be asking themselves when making decisions for their students and classroom.

Reflective practice is not something that is reserved for teachers entering the field. In fact, it may be more beneficial for experienced educators to reflect on their past experiences, creations, and ideas to help them better refine what they do. Reflection is an effective way to identify best practices to maximize the valuable time educators share with students. It is common to create a unit and never see a need to change or make modifications due to past success. Moreover, with constant advances in technology, students having individual laptops, learning management systems becoming the norm and expectation, and Zoom calls replacing classroom meetings, I realized the experienced educator can greatly benefit from using *SOAP Notes* to reflect on student engagement. Applying an intentional effort to reflect is a paramount skill necessary to progress professionally, regardless of the stage of our career.

Overview

The field of education has consistently been asked to adapt to changes in instructional design on a variety of levels. These areas have recently focused on common formative and summative assessments, paired-text reading, student choice, project-based learning, technology integration, pacing, standards-based learning, and many others. As educators question and reflect on why they do what they do, the field of education becomes more thoughtful and thorough in deciding the best practices that will have an impact on student achievement. I have found that reflective practice through *SOAP Notes* is one of these best practices.

My most recent experience using *SOAP Notes* helped me focus on the instructional design strategies I incorporated in my unit on *Beowulf*. As an integrated language arts teacher, I attempt to incorporate a variety of strategies that will allow the students to connect to the literature in their own personal way. The *Beowulf* unit starts with conducting research on historical details of European cultures that helped form and shape what is now called Great Britain. The particular unit of study was taught to a senior-level class that was team taught with an intervention specialist. The class size was relatively small, made up of ten students, but it was filled with many challenges due to the wide spectrum of needs of the students.

From an instructional standpoint, I incorporated a variety of techniques. I used multilevel study guides that provided students opportunities to practice the writing strategy skills we intended to summatively assess at the end of the unit. I incorporated whole class discussions, small group and partnered activities, read aloud sections of the text, and a viewing of the motion picture version of the text, all while incorporating abstract aspects of plot analysis by connecting the *Beowulf* text to concepts related to Joseph Campbell's "Hero's Journey." After reviewing the collective *SOAP Notes* on the instructional design, I identified a variety of approaches I used to keep students engaged. I also noted that there were multiple uses of formative and summative assessment tools to gather information and make decisions on pacing along the way (see Tables 3.1–3.3).

I found areas of strength and areas for improvement. For example, I found room for revision in the area of having students work in small groups and with partners on their learning activities. Additionally, I was able to identify areas where students struggled or lacked engagement; therefore, I will be considering alternative activities for next year. Most importantly, I found that taking the moment to reflect directly after the lesson and

TABLE 3.1 *SOAP Notes*: Beowulf Hero's Journey, Day 12

Evaluation of Instruction (SOAP) *Beowulf: Hero's Journey Epic Narrative Day 1*	By:	Matthew Boggs	Date:	Day 12

_S_	**Subjective**: students' willingness to participate, demeanor, body language, attitude. Teacher's perceptions and reflections
	Students were excited at the opportunity to write creatively. They were interested in details about how creative they could be. Attitude was very positive. A few students appeared a bit nervous about taking creative risks.
_O_	**Observation** of student learning: anecdotal notes
	Students were engaged as we discussed the Hero's Journey templates. I provided multiple examples of different templates that they could generate ideas from. The students liked the idea that they could choose a template and use it to guide their creative thinking.
_A_	**Assessing** student learning: progress monitoring, running records, oral or written comprehension
	The progress monitoring of this lesson will continue over several days as the students work to develop their epic narratives. I will use the provided templates and those generated by student research to evaluate the students' ability to match up with the objectives of the narrative rubric.
_P_	**Planning** for next lesson: use bullet points
	◆ Following the introduction of the project, students will begin to develop a character sketch of strengths and weaknesses of their character, ultimately outlining the ethical challenge that the Hero will have to face. Students will chart out the character's strengths and weaknesses intellectually, emotionally, and ethically. Finally, they will provide a physical description of the character.
Challenges: What challenges did you encounter while working with your students?	
Some students will work at different paces. I foresee some students having a hard time making decisions on their characters and potentially having a hard time deciding how they want to shape the character on the rhetorical level, let alone the physical level.	
Further Learning: What else do you need to know how to do?	
I previously used a few animation apps so the students could attempt to animate their stories. I would like to research more apps that would allow students to create their stories visually, which could possibly inspire or motivate reluctant writers or those that may be struggling to come up with ideas.	

Source: Weaver, J. C., Hartzog, M., Murnen, T., & Bertelsen, C. D. (2019). Bowling Green State University.

TABLE 3.2 *SOAP Notes*: Beowulf Hero's Journey, Day 13

Evaluation of Instruction (SOAP) *Beowulf: Hero's Journey Epic Narrative; Day 2; Character sketch*	By:	Matthew Boggs	Date:	Day 13

S	**Subjective**: students' willingness to participate, demeanor, body language, attitude. Teacher's perceptions and reflections

Students enjoyed creating their characters. Many students were sharing ideas as they developed the strengths and weaknesses on the rhetorical diagram. Several students had a hard time getting started because they had to create a character from scratch.

O	**Observation** of student learning: anecdotal notes

Many students were unsure which area of the rhetorical attributes they should begin with. I provided an example by having them start with the strengths for each rhetorical aspect and then move on to the weaknesses. I found it interesting that many students elected to model many of their character traits after themselves. Many students were reluctant to add weaknesses to their characters and were very thoughtful on what they wanted those weaknesses to be, most notably the intellectual and ethical weaknesses.

A	**Assessing** student learning: progress monitoring, running records, oral or written comprehension

The character sketch worksheet recorded the attributes and showed the students' ability to categorically identify and organize them. This allowed for interesting conversations with the students as they filtered where and why they gave the attributes they did.

P	**Planning** for next lesson: use bullet points

- Following this activity, students will begin to brainstorm challenges that will be fitting for their characters to face.
- Students will be instructed to construct challenges that exploit each rhetorical device, logos, pathos, and ethos. The students will have to consider what the challenge will be and whether or not the hero will overcome the challenge or fail.

Challenges: What challenges did you encounter while working with your students?

Some students will struggle to create their original ideas without scaffolding or guidance. Some students seem to want to have clear directions so they can fill in the box, while others are enjoying the creative freedom and challenge of the activity.

Further Learning: What else do you need to know how to do?

I would like to work on generating more pleasing graphic organizers that will help the students organize their notes and ideas. I need to work on aesthetically pleasing organizers for the students.

Source: Weaver, J. C., Hartzog, M., Murnen, T., & Bertelsen, C. D. (2019). Bowling Green State University.

TABLE 3.3 *SOAP Notes*: Beowulf Hero's Journey, Day 14

Evaluation of Instruction (SOAP) *Beowulf: Hero's Journey Epic Narrative; Day 2; Conflict Creation*	By:	Matthew Boggs	Date:	Day 14
_S_ | **Subjective**: students' willingness to participate, demeanor, body language, attitude. Teacher's perceptions and reflections				
Students were eager to get started and were diligent in their attempt to create challenges for their hero.				
_O_ | **Observation** of student learning: anecdotal notes				
As students were contemplating the types of challenges for their hero to face, they were definitely challenged in how they wanted to link the challenges to each other. I offered the advice of starting with either an emotional or intellectual challenge and to consider whether or not they want the hero to succeed or fail. I provided a plot diagram and had the students fill in where their challenge would fall and identify what type of challenge it would be. All of the students were able to create a challenge covering logos, pathos, and ethos.				
_A_ | **Assessing** student learning: progress monitoring, running records, oral or written comprehension				
Through the students' storyboard, plot diagram, observations, and conferences, I was able to see how each student was planning their hero's tale as well as see how they were developing the plot to allow for the hero to face challenges that were fitting to their character strengths and weaknesses.				
_P_ | **Planning** for next lesson: use bullet points				
◆ Students will begin to draft their hero narratives and begin using the monomyth 12-point outline to organize their hero's journey.				
Challenges: What challenges did you encounter while working with your students?				
Some students may feel challenged to use the guide or to see how they can manipulate and move aspects of the monomyth around within the story to best fit their overall idea. I will assist the students by having them first jot down preliminary ideas for each aspect of the Hero's Journey according to the diagram and then have them consider how they may reorganize the elements to be creative and use elements of foreshadowing, flashbacks, and or flash forwarding to increase tension and elements of dramatic irony.				
Further Learning: What else do you need to know how to do?				
I would like to learn more about programs that would allow the students to illustrate or find animations to provide a visual aid to their writing.				

Source: Weaver, J. C., Hartzog, M., Murnen, T., & Bertelsen, C. D. (2019). Bowling Green State University.

consider my students' immediate needs, I was more prepared for the following lessons. Overall, I was fairly satisfied with the pacing and opportunities for students to work with peers; however, I found that reflecting on student choice for material and incorporating paired texts could be areas that might further benefit my students when I teach this lesson again.

I plan to investigate more content related to the mentor text to allow students to make broad connections with literature and not be solely focused on *Beowulf*. Ultimately, when considering the importance of instructional design and the impact it has on student achievement, *SOAP Notes* is an excellent practice to ask critical questions that shape the decisions I make during the unit planning stages, evaluating the effectiveness of those instructional choices, how it relates to functionality in the classroom, and the overall effectiveness of the learning objectives.

SOAP Notes

As identified by the *S* in the *SOAP Notes* acronym, "Subjective" emphasizes the teachers' perceptions of how the students are participating and showing interest in the classroom activities. When applying this reflective concept to instructional design, a teacher should be asking several questions when creating a lesson or unit plan: *How will students' attitudes be impacted by the types of instructional practices included in the lesson? Will they seem age and developmentally appropriate? Are they rigorous enough to challenge students in a variety of ways, allowing for scaffolding and differentiated instructional opportunities? Will group work versus individual tasks be more of an appropriate method?* These pre-lesson thoughts, along with many others, are significant aspects of what will make a successful lesson for any type of classroom.

Furthermore, educators should continue to observe and note the actual behavior patterns of the students during the lesson. This will help educators recognize types of activities that students openly engage in with meaningful, genuine interest. As part of the *SOAP Notes*, subjective thoughts and opinions of the instructor for how the lesson was received by the students are important to note. The teacher's connection to the success of the lesson or discontent with the lesson's failures should be an essential part of decision-making and reflection.

My "Subjective" notes informed me that several lessons were highly interesting to the students while for others students struggled with engagement. *SOAP Notes* allowed me to see areas I should focus on when I plan the unit again. Many of these subjective thoughts are often lost from year to year when I reteach a lesson because I simply do not remember all the little details of how the students reacted to the content. The *SOAP Notes* strategy supplies a method that allows the educator to retain these subjective thoughts for further review.

To focus on the effectiveness of a lesson, educators can consider the *O* for Observation as part of the *SOAP Notes* strategy. The "Observation of student learning" is essential in a teacher's ability to recognize the formative information that is being displayed throughout the activity. Teachers need to be able to observe when, where, and how students are connecting the content and skills of the lesson and how to apply these learned skills to various tasks. They should also be honest in their reflection, removing bias related to content, or other preconceptions that may cloud the educator's decision in how effective a lesson may be. For instance, if students are simply not engaging with the content because it seems antiquated or otherwise unrelated to the students' interests, it may be time to consider replacing or pairing the text to something more directly related to the students' interests.

My observations of the various lessons I designed identified areas to continue and areas to improve. As I reviewed the notes, I was reminded of many of the little reactions and interests that the students demonstrated during presentations, videos, and activities that helped me consider what to continue and what to change. The daily notation practice required me to stop and think about subtle details that I realized I often overlook when I am focused on creating assessments or reviewing data. The genuine interactions students experience on a daily basis in a classroom are what truly make up the student experience.

Their moods, attitudes, and overall engagement with material are often what they enjoy versus the formative or summative assessments, where I often focus. I appreciated the observations I was able to record as it also helped me remember what the students look forward to or even dread when they enter my classroom.

Along with observing and noting the important learning outcomes of the lesson, finding meaningful assessment strategies within any lesson or unit plan is essential to making decisions about what lessons to follow, revise, or remove. Assessment can be looked at from both formative and summative needs. Because much of what is considered formative assessments can go unrecorded in a classroom setting through the observation of students' work (e.g., in pairs or small groups, discussion with an entire class, or journal writing), taking a moment or two to record the formative assessment outcomes from the daily lessons can serve as a very useful tool.

Recording the formative and summative assessment observation notes provides teachers an opportunity to review the progress of the students in a timely manner. It is a key practice to truly allow student achievement to guide the instruction. Furthermore, actively using formative assessments is essential in making meaningful revisions. In addition, *SOAP Notes* can reflect the outcomes of summative assessments as well. The reflective practice can guide an educator's choice of creating and using summative assessments that demonstrate students' mastery of the learning standards. Reflection on both formative and summative assessments provides opportunities for unique evaluation of strengths and weaknesses in the instructional design of a unit as whole.

The *SOAP Notes* reflective framework asks the teacher to focus on types of assessments, when and how they are using them, and preparation for student success based on the learning targets. These are valid questions that often get overlooked when educators design activities for the classrooms. The negative effects become classroom activities that are perceived as busy work or disconnected from the learning goals. When reflecting on my experience with assessments, I became more aware of the various types of formative and summative assessments I relied on to determine student learning. I found that I was relying on a variety of observation strategies, discussion thread forums, and larger summative projects. This was beneficial in that not only was I able to see the methods of assessment that I most commonly used but also I was able to track how the students were responding to those forms of assessment.

When designing a unit plan, there is a great deal of consideration that involves many details. This may include diversity in texts, differentiated instruction, special needs accommodations, modifications, pacing, content, learning standards, and formative and summative assessments. When using reflective practice for planning, educators are asked to consider how their past experiences and future predictions will account for how they design the learning units for the students. In many cases, reviewing the observations of a lesson can provide clear insight to the educator on areas to improve. In many cases, specific disparities can arise in a more obvious manner than others. Often in the immediate moment of teaching, it is clear that a lesson may not be going as planned or desired. Maybe a group discussion would be better as a partnered activity, maybe a partnered activity would be better as an individual writing prompt, maybe a lecture would be better as a video. The need to reflect and make plans for change is a key component of filling in learning gaps that may be apparent after a lesson has been attempted.

The Planning stage of the *SOAP Notes* strategy for reflective practice is a section where teachers make timely notations about what they can change for the immediate future or even plan to revisit if they choose to continue teaching this lesson at a later date. Asking what action will directly benefit the lesson or will connect the lesson to future lessons is a key component in helping students progress in their learning goals. At first, I struggled to know what I should write in the *Plan* section; however, I began to use this section as a place where I would list what I wanted to do with my students the very next time I saw them. I started to have more seamless transitions from one lesson to the next and began to make subtle changes to my original follow-up lesson based on the notations. I found that a quick evaluation of the *SOAP Notes* on the lesson supplied me with the gist of what I intended to accomplish, an overview of how I felt the lesson went, an account of how the students seemed to respond, the results of the assessment and whether or not I was able to measure what I intended, and the plans I needed to make immediately for the next lesson.

OTES 2.0 Connection

Reflective practice is not something that is new in theory, but it is becoming more and more of a focus for educators when considering how they are evaluated under current teacher evaluation systems. The Ohio Teacher Evaluation System, currently *OTES 2.0*, has a heavy focus on reflective practice. An educator's success and ability to progress hinges directly on their ability to recognize, defend, modify, and revise how they create meaningful units of instruction. These skills, or the lack thereof, are a significant determiner in the overall teacher rating during the evaluation process.

Understanding the students' strengths and weaknesses is important; however, intentionally reflecting on the choices an educator makes has become the focus for professional growth and ensuring that the instruction students receive is well planned, delivered, and reflected upon for future planning purposes. Within the *OTES 2.0* system, there are several domain-related skills that directly connect to reflective practice. These domains are to be critically evaluated and discussed between the teacher and evaluator during their pre- and post-conference meetings. I found becoming skilled in reflective practice helped me prepare to articulate my pre-planned goals for lessons, assess successes and failures within the lesson's delivery, as well as plan to make necessary adjustments moving forward, all of which are part of the *SOAP Notes* reflective practice framework.

I discovered that the pre-conference questions that are part of the OTES 2.0 model ("Pre-Conference Planning") are directly addressed in the *SOAP Notes* reflective practice strategy. The domains of OTES 2.0 include Instructional Planning, Focus for Learning, Knowledge of Students, Instruction Assessment and Delivery, Classroom Environment, Assessment of Student Learning, and Professionalism and Professional Responsibilities. Each aspect of the *SOAP Notes* can be broken down and linked to the domains individually.

Educators can connect the *S* of Subjective to the areas that ask about Instructional Planning, Focus for Learning, and Lesson Delivery. Through these questions, educators are asked to evaluate the instructional strategies they are embracing and how they selected these strategies to best meet the needs of their students based upon what they know about their students. They are also asked to identify the reasoning for choosing specific strategies and how they will meet the needs of all learners.

The *O* of Observation most closely relates to the questions found in the Lesson Delivery and Classroom Environment. Many of these questions are seeking the educator's understanding on how the lesson is inclusive, supportive, and engaging the students. When taking *SOAP Notes*, educators should focus on the feedback the students are providing in their verbal and non-verbal cues along with the information generated from their formative assessments.

The *A*, focused on assessment reflection, is directly connected to questions that fall under the Knowledge of Students and Assessment of Student Learning Questions domains. These questions require the educator to consider what they know about their students, how the assessments are appropriate for the students, and what the overall data shows of students' mastery toward their learning goals.

Lastly, the *P* or Planning section is also related to the Professionalism area of the pre-conference questions. Parts of the plan to revise, modify, re-teach, or remediate can be found in collaboration with colleagues in an effort to scaffold and or support the students with their learning needs. In addition, there may be follow-up action required by a teacher to contact individual students, parents, intervention specialists, or other education service-related individuals.

In attempting to prepare for the evaluation systems that are being used at-large, it is recommended that educators have data showing they are actively reflecting and reviewing throughout the instructional cycle. *SOAP Notes* is an excellent tool that educators can use to not only help guide their teaching for their students' benefit, but also, it can serve as a documented piece of evidence that they are meeting the expectations of their evaluation process.

In addition to the pre-conference questions, a significant part of the OTES 2.0 evaluation is creating a professional growth plan (PGP) and setting personal goals ("Professional Growth Plan"). Under the OTES 2.0 system, there are six domains that an educator can focus on when creating goals for their PGP. Using *SOAP Notes* is a functional way that educators can track their progress and growth as they document their attempt to meet these goals. It can serve as a data point that will support the educator and administrator as they seek to gather evidence when determining the overall rating of the educator.

The application and functionality of *SOAP Notes* for educators at any stage of their career will surely benefit them. This framework is easier when regularly practiced and beneficial information is revealed that most educators do not have the time to collect. The value of information, consideration of practices, and ideas from *SOAP Notes* are integral to collaborative meetings with colleagues and administrators. Whether teachers choose to use *SOAP Notes* for personal use, PGP documentation, or collaborative meetings, *SOAP Notes* become a documented resource for reflection and should continue to be used in the field of education.

TAKE-AWAYS

SOAP Notes **reflective practice helped:**

◆ Identify multiple assessment approaches to gather student learning information
◆ Instructional decision-making
◆ Identify immediate student learning needs
◆ Ask critical questions for instructional effectiveness

Bibliography

Wikipedia, The Free Encyclopedia. (2022 February 20). Hero's journey. Retrieved, February 20, 2022.

Ohio Department of Education. (2021a, August 17). High quality student data. Retrieved, February 20, 2022, from https://education.ohio.gov/Topics/Teaching/Educator-Evaluation-System/Ohio-s-Teacher-Evaluation-System/OTES2.0/High-Quality-Student-Data

Ohio Department of Education. (2021b, January 14). OTES 2.0. Retrieved, February 20, 2022, from https://education.ohio.gov/Topics/Teaching/Educator-Evaluation-System/Ohio-s-Teacher-Evaluation-System/OTES2.0

Ohio Department of Education. (2020a, March 27). Pre-Conference Planning. Retrieved, February 20, 2022, from https://education.ohio.gov/Topics/Teaching/Educator-Evaluation-System/Ohio-s-Teacher-Evaluation-System/OTES2.0/Pre-Conference-Planning-Questions.pdf.aspx?lang-enUS

Ohio Department of Education. (2020b, March 27). Professional Growth Plan. Retrieved, February 20, 2022, from https://education.ohio.gov/Topics/Teaching/Educator-Evaluation-System/Ohio-s-Teacher-Evaluation-System/OTES2.0/Professional-Growth-Plan.pdf.aspx?lang-en-US

Part II

Impact of *SOAP Notes,* Reflection on Instructional Practice

Student Choice and Engagement

4

Self-Reflecting through *SOAP Notes*

A Guide for Teachers Seeking to Find the Best Versions of Themselves for Student Learning

Allison Pamer

GETTING TO KNOW THE AUTHOR

♦ High school English teacher
♦ 4th year of teaching
♦ Career Tech High School

Four years and a pandemic later, I know who I am as a teacher. I worked incredibly hard to get there. Through listening to podcasts, being a part of teacher groups, working with mentors, and a lot of trial and error in my own classroom, I learned that I love student-centered learning. It is the core to my teaching philosophy and who I am when I go to school each day. I dedicated

DOI: 10.4324/9781003493464-8

myself to providing my students with interactive activities, projects, and lessons that focus on engaging all learning styles with an emphasis on student choice. Just because I know who I am as a teacher does not mean that I have everything figured out and I never have to plan a new lesson ever again. I plan new lessons and activities daily. Many succeed, and many fail. I self-reflect, identify what to change or what went well, then try again.

With the opportunity of growth comes a great responsibility to use self-reflective teaching practices to ensure that plans are intentional and not chaotic. Students deserve consistency and thoughtful planning and reflection throughout their journey of growth. Self-reflective teaching practices are a crucial component to any teacher's journey of growth as well. A simple, effective, and tangible way to monitor reflective teaching is through *SOAP Notes*.

SOAP Notes are self-guided notes that can be used daily, weekly, by unit, or even by class for a teacher to analyze their teaching practices in a thoughtful way. These notes are essential for any teacher looking to analyze what is working, what is not, and what changes need to be made to establish growth in learning. Through these notes, teachers will reflect on a lesson by analyzing the *S*ubjective (student's willingness to participate, demeanor, body language, attitude, teacher's perceptions and reactions), *O*bservations of student learning, *A*ssessment of student learning (progress monitoring, running records, oral or written comprehension), *P*lanning for the next lesson, challenges from the lesson or with students, and notes for further learning.

Across a three-week unit of study, I used *SOAP Notes* to analyze my Puritanism and Dark Romanticism units with my 11th grade students. I teach at an amazing career center. By teaching at a career center, I have been granted countless opportunities to enhance my teaching abilities because of the demographics of the students. Many traditional high school teachers assign readings outside of school; ask students to sit through long, traditional lectures; and have them write essay after essay. Teaching at a career center brought me into contact with an overwhelming majority of students who are kinesthetic learners.

I learned very quickly that in order to engage my students, I needed to understand who they were as learners, how I can relate our curriculum to their futures, and that my teaching needed to address all learning styles in order to be an effective English teacher. I loved this challenge, and it developed my philosophy of student-centered learning. *SOAP Notes* have helped me identify how I can continue to turn traditional curriculum such as Puritanism and Romanticism into relevant, engaging, and hands-on learning opportunities for my students.

Before beginning these *SOAP Notes*, I identified an area of growth for myself that I wanted to track through this reflective teaching practice. My goal was to integrate more opportunities for student choice into my curriculum. Student choice is essential for effective differentiation, appealing to all learning styles, and ensuring that we are giving every student the opportunity to show their knowledge in a way that emphasizes their own individual strengths and talents, but student choice can be challenging to master as a teacher. Not only do teachers need to create multiple options for projects or activities that appeal to different learning styles, but also they need to predict how long each project option will take to ensure that students are being challenged equally. Additionally, these various project options should assess students on the same skills but through different mediums. It is no easy task, but using *SOAP Notes* helped me reflect on the student choice opportunity and gave me time to reflect on what was working and what needed refinement.

Each day that I wrote these *SOAP Notes*, I focused on scaffolding and creating lessons that appealed to all learning styles. At the end of both my Puritanism and Romanticism units, I challenged myself to create new opportunities for student choice through various summative projects. Through this implementation, I analyzed student behavior, participation, engagement, takeaways, patterns, assessments, and planned for future lessons based on my findings. *SOAP Notes* took me out of my head as a teacher. Rather than focusing solely on my lesson, I reflected intentionally on students' behaviors and connection to learning. My students' feedback, observations, participation, and engagement helped me to determine where to go next.

In my Puritanism unit, I taught *The Crucible* with my students. At the end of the play, I implemented my first student choice final project. These options included two essay options, a mask assignment, and a meme writing assignment. To support my students who chose the essay options, I provided each with a brochure for writing essays, set up one-on-one conferences, checkpoints, and assisted with the writing process. The second project option was for students to create a mask for a character in *The Crucible*. These masks were based on themes, symbols, and quotes in the play. Students could create these masks through drawing, using technology to create a digital version, or designing a real mask using paint and other supplies, making this a hands-on project. There was also a writing component as well. The final project option was a meme project. Based on themes and conflicts in the play, students created their own meme and completed a corresponding writing assignment.

> On day 2 of this project, under student observation (O) in my *SOAP Notes*, I noted:

> The difficult thing about student choice is finding projects that take the same amount of time as one another to help manage time. A pattern emerging is that some students are close to finishing while others are in the beginning stages. Particularly, the meme project is moving quicker than the essays or mask project. I am still working on improving this as I implement student choice into my plans.

Based on these observations, I noted in my *SOAP Notes* that my planning included, "Meet with each student individually about their project progress, pair essay writers with one another to proofread and edit, and ensure that meme projects follow requirements and corresponding writing assignment includes textual evidence and that peer editing takes place."

The next day, I made a note to meet with each student that finished their projects before everyone else. Most students that fell into this category had the meme project option. After meeting with students, I observed in my *SOAP Notes* that, "Many students that were moving too fast in the meme project option did not have textual evidence in their writing responses." As a result, "I made sure to meet with each student one-on-one to give feedback and help students with corrections. I also created a peer editing checklist to help students revise their writing." This intervention not only slowed down students who rushed through the project but also supported them in making better changes to their project. Ultimately, based on my *SOAP Notes*, I decided that the two essay options and mask assignment were successful student choice options, but I will switch out the meme project for something more rigorous next year.

In my next unit, Dark Romanticism, I used *SOAP Notes* to guide my students to our final project where I once again implemented student choice. This time, students only had three options. Option one was for students to create Poe's house listings and use persuasive techniques to sell the houses in his stories (where murders occurred). The second option was a traditional essay. The third option was to write their own spooky short story using Dark Romantic elements and a suspenseful mood or tone. Students wrote their choices on an index card and gave them to me along with how I can support them through the project and if they had any questions. I taught a mini-lesson about persuasive techniques for the house listings project, provided students who chose the traditional essay with a helpful essay writing brochure, and gave graphic organizers to the students who chose the spooky short story project. Based on my one-on-one conferences and observations of my students through *SOAP Notes*, I noticed right away that the house listings project was moving faster than the other two writing options.

On day 14 of my *SOAP Notes* under *Challenges*, I noted:

The project ideas I came up with are new to me, so I am not sure how they will work with my students yet or if the two projects will take the same amount of time. I may need to add more to the house listing project option if students get through it quicker than the short story.

The next day, this project option was still moving too fast, which I again noted as a challenge in my *SOAP Notes*. Under further learning, I decided that in order to solve this problem, "I need to add a part 2. I will use a creative element to appeal to visual and kinesthetic learning styles." I sat and reflected about how I could further students' learning while also appealing to their learning styles. I thought about adding a creative element since students already used persuasive writing. Furthermore, I wanted to transfer these skills of persuasive writing into a different medium to make the additional part of the project meaningful.

With this in mind, I decided to have students with the house listings project also design a real estate brochure using their modes of persuasion and technology/hand drawing to bring their house listings to life. I recorded this idea under my plans for future learning on my *SOAP Notes*. Now, instead of students using persuasive writing to sell a fictional and abstract house, they were getting the opportunity to illustrate the house and use their persuasive writing to channel into a more kinesthetic project. This solution evened out the timing of the other projects and worked well. During the time I reflected on future lessons, I decided, I will reuse Part 2 of the project again during my next Dark Romanticism unit.

Reflective practices, such as *SOAP Notes*, encourages us to step back as a teacher and observe how lessons influence student learning. *SOAP Notes* will give us the tools to constantly reflect and grow as a teacher. Whether it is through assessment data, observing students' demeanors and body language, participation, patterns in student learning, or feedback from students, *SOAP Notes* connect us to our students.

With *SOAP Notes*, teachers can have the opportunity to intentionally identify how students interacted with the lesson and what teachers can do to revise and strengthen the lesson. The best part of reflective practices such as *SOAP Notes* is that we have the power to reflect and revise and continue to take calculated risks to ensure that students are learning.

SOAP Notes have been a very helpful reflective practice for my own learning about my instruction. I am constantly evolving as an educator with every new class that comes before me.

Each year I teach, I focus on new goals for myself as a teacher. Student choice was my goal this year, and it is a difficult method to master. It takes practice, a great deal of thought and effort, and reflection to run smoothly. As I continue to reflect on my own teaching practices, I also learn how to problem-solve quickly when my observations and patterns show me that something in my plans needs refinement. With each new student choice opportunity I provide my students, I am growing, too. I am learning how to manage my projects' timing, matching rigor across all project options, selecting projects that align with my students' learning styles, and providing my students with the resources to succeed based on their individual strengths and talents.

Being an effective teacher does not mean that we have everything figured out at once. It means that we are willing to reflect and grow alongside our students, for our students. It means that we are getting out of our comfort zones to try new ideas that have been proven to help students shine. As Mortimer Adler once said, "The purpose of learning is growth, and our minds, unlike our bodies, can continue growing as we continue to live." *SOAP Notes* is a reflective practice that gives teachers the tools to be vulnerable and analyze their own teaching practices through their students. In a world where teaching is constantly changing and evolving, *SOAP Notes* can be a powerful tool.

TAKE-AWAYS

SOAP Notes **reflective practice helped:**

◆ Teachers take risks
◆ Teachers focus on specific instructional strategies (e.g., student choice, conferences)
◆ Teachers be vulnerable

5

Reflective Practice

The Root of Quality Teaching

Gabrielle Dendinger

GETTING TO KNOW THE AUTHOR

♦ 8th grade ELA teacher
♦ 3rd year of teaching
♦ Urban, high need middle school

I chose to focus my *SOAP Notes* on a poetry unit. I honestly had never taught poetry so explicitly in my two previous years of teaching. Nonetheless, upon reflection, my co-teacher and I both felt the poetry unit was our best unit this school year. Reflective practice is powerful. Integrating *SOAP Notes* reflective practice into a daily routine will make a positive difference for students, and that is something we all want.

SOAP Notes reflections have impacted how I hold students accountable for independent reading in the classroom. At my school, the literacy coach emphasized the need for students to read independently for 15 minutes per day. It is important to note that students were given the choice in what they read.

DOI: 10.4324/9781003493464-9

Each individual was able to choose a text they preferred in terms of genre, length, and level. We discussed the importance of just right books and how to go about choosing a book, but students ultimately had the ability to self-select their text. Some students chose a book from the classroom library while other students utilized our school library. Other students chose to read informational texts from a website on their Chromebook. Also, I did not require students to read an entire novel if they decided the book they had previously chosen was not for them. Regardless of the text selected, students independently read to begin class each day.

Implementation of *SOAP Notes*

I used *SOAP Notes* to reflect on the effectiveness of independent reading and student participation. I found that student engagement with their independent reading text varied. Some students did great entering the classroom and getting their independent self-selected reading book out to begin reading. However, a handful of students needed to be verbally reminded of the expectation multiple times within the 15 minutes.

Independent Reading

I witnessed and recorded students staring off into space and staring down at their desk instead of reading their texts. When writing my *SOAP Notes* and analyzing students' willingness to participate, their demeanor, body language, and attitude, I decided that I would like independent reading time to be more focused for students. I felt students needed a purpose for their independent reading, so, in response, my co-teacher and I developed an activity for students to engage with for a total of two weeks that helped guide students during their independent reading time. The assignment created consisted of five parts. In part one, students were prompted to describe the setting in their book with textual evidence to support their thinking. Then, students were asked to describe the main characters in their book using textual evidence. Next, students were asked to articulate why they chose their book through at least three sentences. Fourth, students were asked to apply a skill we had been working on with texts in class, annotating, by creating three annotations for their text. Lastly, students were tasked with creating a logical prediction about something that may occur in the plot of the story. The creation of this assignment assisted me in holding students accountable for their independent reading and is a direct product of my reflective practice using *SOAP Notes*.

As time went on, the independent reading expectations became a routine for students. In my *SOAP Notes*, I noted students' willingness to begin class by participating in 15 minutes of independent reading had become a well instilled routine. I saw a similar effort from students on the tenth day. I further reflected that I felt students were behaving as expected because the routine and expectation was set and it did not waiver. Students knew what to do during the first 15 minutes of class each day and had risen to the occasion. *SOAP Notes* reflective practice influenced my day-to-day instruction greatly.

Student Participation

Furthermore, student participation was an area of focus within my *SOAP Notes*. On the second day of the poetry unit, I noticed that students were not overly engaged with the guided slides I utilized to introduce the poetry genre, even though many educational videos were used throughout to visually show examples of poetic devices.

In response to a lack of engagement with guided slide notes, my co-teacher and I planned to conduct class using three small groups the following day. He led one group of figurative language instruction; there was an independent group where students completed two EdPuzzles focused on building background knowledge around famous American poet Emily Dickinson, and I led one group that completed the first read of an Emily Dickinson poem and began surface level analysis of the poem.

Impact on Student Learning

Based on my analysis of *SOAP Notes*, I found that small group station rotations positively impacted student learning. One student specifically told me that he really enjoyed diving into poetry through the stations we set up. He mentioned discussing the poem in a small group helped him to understand the complexity of Dickinson's word choice. I also noticed a student who often had his head down during instruction participating actively through small group instruction. I continued to be encouraged by students who often do not participate in whole class instruction participating actively through small group instruction. There were two specific students who started to shine in small groups when their engagement in the past had been lacking tremendously. On the third day of small group poetry instruction, I reflected on one major highlight for me: A student who never participated in whole class instruction participated in my small group vocabulary instruction.

It was very impactful to see just how much small group instruction was able to benefit students in their learning of a challenging genre. Based on the clear examples of students experiencing poetry instruction more positively through small group instruction as opposed to whole class instruction, my co-teacher and I continued to implement small group instruction going forward to better meet our students' needs.

Impact on Instruction

Using *SOAP Notes* to reflect on my day-to-day lessons impacted my own learning about instruction. I found that the *Challenges* and *Further Learning* sections of the *SOAP Notes* template served to challenge me as a teacher. Sometimes questioning ourselves and our teaching practices is hard to do. While challenging, the result of reflection is worth it. Looking back on this process, I wholeheartedly believe practicing reflective practice for three weeks made me a better educator for my students.

One main area of growth that I saw within myself as an educator refers to student engagement. From the beginning of the school year, student engagement has been one of the biggest challenges with my students. More than any other school year, I saw students who were exhausted and unprepared for school daily. I looked out into my classroom as I was teaching and saw students with their heads down upon their desks as opposed to making eye contact with me or raising their hands to participate in class discussions. Not every student had their head down, not even a majority of students did, but some students were not engaged daily, and that was something I took special notice of all year. As a result, I wrote about student engagement often in the Challenges section of the *SOAP Notes* template.

As I began teaching poetry through small group instruction, I struggled to balance small group and partner application time for students. When comparing the two, I noticed that student learning did not seem to be as strong in partner pairs as it did in small groups. One element that I noticed was students had a hard time getting focused and started on their work when in partners as opposed to learning through guided small groups. This led me to question how to balance station rotation instruction and partner application for students.

Another engagement challenge I faced was when students needed to work collaboratively in teams. For example, I planned for students to engage in a figurative language competition. Students worked in teams of four to work through the challenge. As I monitored group progress, I noticed certain students carrying the entire team during the figurative language competition. It was discouraging to see, especially when the point of the competition was to collaborate and learn together. I wanted to see more collaboration and student buy-in through that activity.

This led me to question how I ensure all students participate in team activities and one student does not carry the team.

Furthermore, a colleague shared that activity with me after it went well for her students. I wonder why my students did not take to it the same way? This led me to acknowledge the need to know how my colleague grouped her students and presented the competition to her students.

I don't have the answers to many of the further learning questions the *SOAP Notes* template prompted me to ponder. But that's okay. I find strength in the depth of the questions I posed. I took pride in the questions I posed as I believed they showed my care and concern for my students and their engagement in ELA. I believe the further learning questions I am still working through continue to mold me into a better teacher for my students.

The *SOAP Notes* process inspired me to make some other reflections that I wanted to continue to work through as an educator. First, enrichment is an area I continued to see as an area of growth for me. In the co-taught classroom, my focus was usually more on the lower achieving students than the higher achieving ones. What were the best ways to challenge higher achieving students without simply adding more work to their load? Second, I often felt pressure from administration to "teach to the bell," but failing to give students adequate time to complete activities backfires. For example, I wanted students to complete an exit ticket, but it was rushed, so I did not have total participation in completion because students did not have enough time in class to complete the task. This highlighted an area of growth for me as I tried to navigate "teaching to the bell" and providing students with enough time to showcase their learning.

In closing, working through the process of engaging in *SOAP Notes* reflective practice has absolutely impacted my students, classroom, and instruction in a positive way. I am able to better accommodate my students' needs when I take the time to engage in thoughtful reflective practice after teaching new lessons and trying new activities. I believe in the power of reflective practice. I challenge you to add *SOAP Notes* reflective practice into your planning routine. I feel this addition will allow you to see your instruction evolve and flourish for the betterment of student learning.

TAKE-AWAYS

SOAP Notes **reflective practice helped:**

- ◆ Implementation of independent reading time
- ◆ Teacher's ability to address and support student learning
- ◆ Student learning during small group work
- ◆ Student participation
- ◆ Teacher's learning about instruction

6

Teaching the "Human" Side of Education

Emily Hamric

GETTING TO KNOW THE AUTHOR

♦ High school English teacher and College Credit Plus
♦ 6th year of teaching
♦ Career tech high school

Because my district is a career center, my students come to me with vastly different knowledge bases and skill sets that can make it difficult to determine need and interest throughout the school year. A thriving career center also means that our classes tend to be fairly large (my smallest class this year has 23 students), with a body of students in each class who, most often, don't know each other very well, if at all. My students' differing skill sets and their timidity with each other makes group work, presentations, class discussions, and anything that isn't seat-based work incredibly difficult to achieve successfully, especially during the first semester. This type of environment can also make it difficult for me to reflect on their interest and engagement in a lesson

DOI: 10.4324/9781003493464-10

because the students are not very willing to openly share their interests or ideas early in the school year.

I completed my *SOAP Notes* unit of study over 15 days, and because my students were still pretty unfamiliar with each other at this point in the school year, I chose to complete my project in one of my senior English classes that is a bit more outgoing and would provide more verbal and nonverbal feedback than my other classes. I hoped that this class would provide more observational assessment for me to use for my *SOAP Notes* reflection, and it turned out to be the correct choice. This group of students got to know each other quickly at the beginning of the school year, which made my reflective teaching practices much easier to accomplish. The unit I chose to focus on for my *SOAP Notes* was a scary story unit that focused on vocabulary analysis and use, as well as figurative language analysis and assessment. I tend to have pretty positive reactions to this unit each year, so I was excited to more closely observe my senior students throughout this unit.

Upon my first reflection, I immediately noticed that *SOAP Notes* are different from other teacher reflections that I have used because the *SOAP Notes* model encouraged me to pay attention to my students' demeanor, body, language, and attitudes throughout class as part of the Subjective section of the template. As a teacher, I tend to pay attention to these things without the need for specific reflection, but I don't tend to write them down, and that is where writing *SOAP Notes* impacted my instructional choices and provided the most reflection.

One of the greatest benefits of *SOAP Notes* is the specific place to note students' demeanor, body language, and attitudes for that day's lesson. I always want my students to be engaged in my lessons and enjoy their learning, but having to really pay attention to my students' behaviors in regard to my lesson choices was eye-opening for me. I was definitely paying more attention to the reactions from all of my students since I had to write them down in the Subjective part of the *SOAP Notes* chart. Reading back through my notes from the three weeks, I noticed that I was often surprised by my students' reactions to an assignment or activity. For instance, my first two lessons were simple reflections on my students' demeanors while taking a school-mandated reading diagnostic. I always know that my students absolutely despise any form of mandated testing, but writing it down and really reflecting on their attitudes toward the diagnostic was disheartening.

I was surprised by just how many students had negative reactions to this, as opposed to neutral reactions. One reaction from a student was even severe, as I noted: "There were several moans and groans about it, and one student slammed her laptop lid closed when I mentioned that they should wait to start the assessment until everyone was ready." Yikes. Looking back through those first two sets of notes, it does make me re-evaluate the importance and necessity of mandated testing, especially when students have been inundated with it since they started school as kindergartners. *SOAP Notes* are great for reflective teaching day-to-day but also provide observational data for broader questions in education. As disheartening as it is to re-read my students' reactions to an assessment like this, it is incredibly satisfying and enlightening to re-read their reactions to the lessons that were planned in the following days.

In the following days after the mandatory assessment, I introduced my students to a Spooky Story unit that would culminate in a Spooky Story curation project and presentation. However, before I could introduce the project and set my students loose with it, I wanted to make sure that they had a strong grasp of all of the figurative language that I would be expecting them to be able to identify and assess throughout the project. I was a bit unsure about introducing this project to them at all because figurative language is something that most of them have learned and relearned over the course of several school years, so I anticipated that I would receive some groans of despair when I introduced the unit. The first thing I did to introduce the unit was read *The Legend of Sleepy Hollow* by Washington Irving with my class. I wanted to introduce a high level text that was engaging and would challenge my students' vocabulary and figurative language skills.

To my surprise, my students were excited to read the story and even more excited about the scary story project in general.

I even wrote in my *SOAP Notes*, "I was actually surprised at the outbursts of excitement when I announced it," and re-reading that, I remember feeling very excited about the future of the project over the next couple of weeks. As we began reading *The Legend of Sleepy Hollow*, my students were engaged in the plot but a bit wary of the language used in the "old-timey" story. I anticipated this and provided a vocabulary strategy called word gradients to help them find synonyms for unfamiliar words. This strategy seemed to resonate with most of my students, and in the Assessing section of my *SOAP Notes*, I noted that the students did a nice job on their word gradients and that I would analyze their most-used words for the gradients to determine a vocabulary pre- and post-assessment.

I realize, looking back at my notes from this particular lesson, that I pretty much abandoned my quest for figurative language analysis in favor of vocabulary instruction and analysis. I noted in the Further Learning section of my *SOAP Notes* that, "I also severely underestimated the vocabulary instruction needed for my students to read this story" that led to my mid-lesson change in plans from figurative language instruction to only vocabulary instruction for that day. Regardless, my *SOAP Notes* are filled with excitement because my students continued to be engaged and motivated to read *The Legend of Sleepy Hollow* and complete the scary story unit. Writing down my own adaptations and my students' reactions to those adaptations is helpful in showing me that we are all able to adapt to change, and that my lessons don't always need to go as initially planned to be successful. Had I not taken *SOAP Notes* during this particular unit, I probably would have forgotten all about this adaptation, and I wouldn't be able to appreciate my own flexibility in teaching, nor my students' excited response to something that was a bit challenging for them.

Something else that I noticed while re-reading my *SOAP Notes* from this unit was my reflection on how student choice in education impacts a student's engagement and learning. As I observed my students completing their Spooky Story curation projects, I noticed how engaged most of my students were with the stories that they had found and analyzed to complete their projects. One of the goals of a curation project, outside of learning to analyze and assess work, is that students take agency over their own learning through choosing what they want to analyze and assess for the project. As I observed my students finishing up their projects, I noted in the Observation section of my *SOAP Notes*:

> I am fascinated by how much the students seemed to have learned by just engaging in material that is interesting to them. I think providing student choice is so beneficial to creating engagement and true learning, and this project proves that. I have heard a lot of conversations based around figurative language, characterization, and plot.

While I know how valuable student choice is to learning, it is incredibly useful to actually write down the value that I saw in it as a reflection on the lesson, and then be able to return to that reflection as a reminder of lessons or units that work and why they work. I think that one of the most beneficial aspects to any type of reflection is the ability to go back and re-read the reflections in preparation for a new unit or as a way to help focus one's teaching.

While I do think that there is much to be gained from using *SOAP Notes* for specific reflective teaching practices, there are a couple of drawbacks to this particular type of reflection that caught my attention as I used *SOAP Notes*. While I loved the specific reflection on students' reactions and demeanors during a lesson, I feel that *SOAP Notes* are lacking when it comes to the *Assessing* and *Planning* aspects of a lesson, only because I had trouble connecting these each day without a more structured guideline for reflection.

SOAP Notes is a great teacher reflection tool if that teacher is looking for something that is a more informal way of reflecting on his or her lessons and planning. I appreciated the informality of *SOAP Notes* as it did not feel like a burden to complete them. I was able to adapt based on student interest and engagement. Ultimately, they helped me to create a unit that was well assessed and well enjoyed by my students. Overall, I plan to continue using *SOAP Notes* in the future. My teaching definitely benefited from using *SOAP Notes* reflections particularly because they encouraged me to appreciate my students' engagement, enjoyment, frustrations, and adaptability.

The unit that I used for my *SOAP Notes* unit of study provided me with clear reflection on my students' interests and engagement, but also with reflection on the value of teacher adaptability and student choice. I think that one of the biggest values of this style of reflection is having to focus on student engagement and being able to go back and re-read reflections as I continue to plan for the school year.

SOAP Notes help teachers to pay attention to not only the "education" side of their job but also the "human" side. In fact, I would argue that the *SOAP Notes* template pays more attention to the human side of the job. For teachers like me, who tend to pay more attention to the academic side of education, *SOAP Notes* are a welcome engagement with the side of education that touches my students' hearts and minds equally. I will continue to use *SOAP Notes* throughout my teaching career, especially when I feel that I am struggling to engage or relate to a class. I have found *SOAP Notes* to be highly effective in helping me adapt my teaching practices appropriately and relate to my students in ways that help them engage in their own learning.

TAKE-AWAYS

SOAP Notes reflective practice helped:

◆ Teachers adapt teaching practices
◆ Teachers address the academic and human sides of instruction
◆ Teachers be flexible
◆ Teachers support engagement, motivation, and gauge student learning
◆ Support student agency and choice

Application of *SOAP Notes*

7

Trusting Yourself and Your Students

Myka Chavez-EnYart

GETTING TO KNOW THE AUTHOR

♦ High school English teacher
♦ 6th year of teaching
♦ Urban high school

As teachers, one of the things we hear most often is the importance of reflecting on our teaching day to day. It's something we hear from professors as we train to be teachers, it's something we hear as we move through our first years as educators and while completing RESA, and often, it's a requirement or strong recommendation from our principals who double as evaluators. Despite constant reminders, and though many of us can agree on the benefits of daily reflection, it often gets neglected day to day and pushed down the overwhelming list of tasks we must complete.

Many of us already put a tremendous amount of pressure on ourselves to have the most engaging, inclusive, and data-driven lesson plans, so reflecting can sometimes leave us with one more

DOI: 10.4324/9781003493464-12

thing to criticize about ourselves, focusing only on what we could have or should have done better each day. However, I'm here to advocate for practicing daily reflection. I've learned, even as a busy high school teacher with multiple preps, through using *SOAP Notes* I *can* find time for reflection, and that my reflection notes *can* do more for my students and me than simply discourage me and leave me feeling like I'm not doing enough. Daily reflection has improved the trust between my students and me and has given me more confidence in my lesson delivery.

To start, I should provide some context about where I was before starting daily reflection. Our English department has been in the process of adopting a new curriculum framework, consisting of set units that we use to frame our teaching throughout the year. Each unit centers around a central text, and that is how we've determined which texts to teach at each grade level the past several years.

This particular school year, I taught only one section of 12th grade English. I realized that sometimes this was the class that would get the least of my energy and attention when it came to lesson planning each week. This wasn't sitting right with me— first, because it was my duty as their teacher to ensure I was giving these students an equal amount of effort and thought, and second, to give credit where credit is due, all of my senior students in that first period class passed first quarter and held themselves accountable for getting caught up on their work even when absent or a little sleepy. They were a very quiet group of students, but on the whole responsible, hard-working, and eager to learn, so I was often assuming they didn't need much guidance from me. This is why I chose them as my focus group, in hopes that reflecting daily on these lessons would help me identify areas to improve engagement and hold myself accountable for giving this deserving class more of my energy and attention.

My planning period was the second hour, which was perfect to hold me accountable because I *did* have some work time available to complete the *SOAP Notes* reflection form immediately following my first period lesson each day. Having a designated time to reflect really helped me to follow through with completing the *SOAP Notes* consistently and fall into a pattern with them. I completed my *SOAP Notes* reflections each school day over the course of three school weeks, which amounted to 12 days of teaching. In these three weeks, I learned a lot about my students and myself.

First, one focus for my reflection was paying closer attention to how well my simple approach to teaching the novel *Sing, Unburied, Sing* by Jesmyn Ward was working with this group of students. My simple approach was basically that students would follow along with the audiobook of the novel and take strategic notes, we would discuss, then students would have chapter questions and a discussion board to answer. What I wanted to know was—*Were they engaged in these lessons? Did they seem to be learning without my strict guidance? Were they willing to share their thoughts regarding the novel?* I included some entries from my *SOAP Notes* that exemplify my concerns that students were not effectively engaging in the novel lessons (see Table 7.1).

These SOAP note entries were indicative of an overall sense I had that students were not getting as much out of these lessons as they could be, leaving me to wonder how I could use these takeaways to help improve my instruction in a way that would encourage participation more. I then realized a potentially problematic pattern across my comments. I realized that each time I noted a challenge in students' engagement or learning, I was putting the accountability and work toward improving those things entirely on myself. "I" was going to put in extra work to encourage each individual student to participate, "I" was going to type up the answers for them because they didn't do it themselves, "I" was sad that a few students, out of 26 total, verbally expressed a dislike for the book, as if "I" chose it or wrote it and as if students had to like a book to learn from it.

At this point, I realized I had to reframe my mindset and approach. It wasn't productive for me to just add extra work for myself to hold every individual student accountable when they knew what they were supposed to be doing to engage with the lessons. Besides, one thing I'd always wanted to improve about my instruction was putting more responsibility on students to take charge of their own learning. This was all compounded with the fact that when I took a closer look at my *SOAP Notes* with

TABLE 7.1 *SOAP Notes*: Challenge

Evaluation of Instruction (SOAP)	By:		Date:	
<u>S</u>	**Subjective**: students' willingness to participate, demeanor, body language, attitude. Teacher's perceptions and reflections			
Students actually seemed more alert today than they have in a while. This might be due to the new quarter and a day off prior; they were jotting notes (at least the majority) about background on the novel despite it being optional, and all students were awake and off their phones.				
<u>O</u>	**Observation** of student learning: anecdotal notes			
I think students were able to gain background knowledge of the setting, author, and purpose behind the novel *Sing, Unburied, Sing*. In particular, based on when I saw the most students jotting notes, they seemed most intrigued by the pictures of the bayou setting and the idea of ghosts being in the book.				
<u>A</u>	**Assessing** student learning: progress monitoring, running records, oral or written comprehension			
It was a short class period for background notes, so I did not progress monitor beyond observing student behavior.				
<u>P</u>	**Planning** for next lesson: use bullet points			
◆ I will ask students to share some of what they wrote down today and to review the info and have it fresh in their minds when we read				
Challenges: What challenges did you encounter while working with your students?				
My challenge was that I have never taught this novel before and just recently read it for the first time. I lacked background info myself, which made me go through the background info maybe a little too fast for the students because I wasn't practiced in where to stop and elaborate, what to emphasize, and so on.				
Further Learning: What else do you need to know how to do?				
Figure out a way to increase participation in class discussions. One idea: use white boards.				

Source: Weaver, J. C., Hartzog, M., Murnen, T., & Bertelsen, C. D. (2019). Bowling Green State University.

a slightly different frame of mind, I realized that the majority of students *were* engaging in the learning and lessons (see Table 7.2). Their engagement looked different because their learning preferences were largely intrapersonal. One specific indication of this was that for each chapter, students were required to answer a discussion question about it using Canvas. They were

TABLE 7.2 *SOAP Notes*: Subjective

Evaluation of Instruction (SOAP)			Date:	
S	**Subjective**: students' willingness to participate, demeanor, body language, attitude. Teacher's perceptions and reflections			
Out of 21 students present today, as we read and followed along with audio for the novel, I only counted three who were off-task. They seemed engaged with the novel, and one student even made a comment about the gruesomeness of the first chapter because of all the detail in the descriptions.				
O	**Observation** of student learning: anecdotal notes			
Although students followed along with the novel today, I'm not sure they started doing much analysis or critical thinking about the literary elements within the novel yet. They also had pre-reading questions to complete before we started the novel, but these were personal questions about them that did relate to the book. However, I don't think they've started to make the connection between the questions I asked them and the content of Chapter 1 yet.				
A	**Assessing** student learning: progress monitoring, running records, oral or written comprehension			
17/21 students completed and submitted the pre-reading questions to Canvas on time today. This is more of a progress monitoring assignment as far as completing a task. We'll need to get a little farther in the unit for me to have assessments of students' ELA skills.				
P	**Planning** for next lesson: use bullet points			
<ul><li>We are going to re-read the first nine pages tomorrow, but with some specific guidelines for points of analysis I want students to take note of this time around. This will help them start to be mindful of analysis as they read, and to read with a purpose, rather than just sit and listen, which is what they did today.</li><li>We will talk about any connections they recognize from the previous lesson on background for the novel (we were supposed to do this today but ran out of time) and/or how they're seeing the pre-reading questions I asked them become relevant.</li></ul>				
Challenges: What challenges did you encounter while working with your students?				
For the students who were off-task, I documented they were off-task, and that's usually my approach after I've redirected them a few times. However, I think I should do a little more to check in with them and make sure they're on-task during the lesson.				
Further Learning: What else do you need to know how to do?				
Figure out a good system for annotating to teach the students because they can't mark in the actual novel copies, but I want them to take note of things they notice as they read.				

Source: Weaver, J. C., Hartzog, M., Murnen, T., & Bertelsen, C. D. (2019). Bowling Green State University.

to complete an initial post, and then also respond to one peer. In this forum, students were engaging in really detailed discussions that included evidence from the text, and that was the goal.

However, I still wasn't hearing from them during whole group instruction, so upon review of my reflections, I was able to narrow down the struggle from "students are disengaged" to "students are struggling with active participation in the verbal class discussions we were trying to have about the novel." Instead of conceding that I just wouldn't ever hear from more than two students during discussion, and instead of putting the work of holding every individual student accountable on myself, I decided to design a lesson in which students could participate during class without having to verbally share answers and see if that would yield more active participation from students (see Table 7.3).

TABLE 7.3 *SOAP Notes: Further Learning.*

7.3a			
Evaluation of Instruction (SOAP)	By:		Date:
S	**Subjective**: students' willingness to participate, demeanor, body language, attitude. Teacher's perceptions and reflections		
	I only saw one student with their book closed today. The majority of other students, 23/24 of them, were on task, following along in their novels with the audio and taking notes in their notebooks based on the bullet points of things I asked them to look for. The students also seemed willing to participate in the discussion today. I think the directions for what to look for ahead of time helped, and they didn't feel put on the spot, so they were able to share answers they already wrote down and had time to think about.		
Q	**Observation** of student learning; anecdotal notes		
	Students understood where to look for answers to the analysis questions because I directed them with page numbers. When I looked around when we got to pages 1 and 6, I saw many students writing down answers and ideas to the analysis questions. Based on our discussion, I think students were starting to relate with the characters and make some connections between the background we discussed during Wednesday's class and the pre-reading questions from Thursday. They mentioned that Jojo's family dynamic in the book was one that a lot of people experience but were able to recognize that it does not fit within the "traditional nuclear" mold. They also detected that the tone of the novel so far is a little sad because it's Jojo's birthday and Pop is busy, his grandma is sick, and his mother seems neglectful of him. I think they were making meaning from the story so far, but I should have asked if they liked it or not.		

(Continued)

TABLE 7.3 (Continued)

$\underline{A}$	**Assessing** student learning: progress monitoring, running records, oral or written comprehension

Students were assessed today through oral comprehension. We had a discussion about their answers to the analysis questions I asked them to take notes on for the first seven pages and based on how the pre-reading background information and pre-reading questions were showing up so far. I heard from about five different students, which is more than usual for this group. They touched on each of the points I'd hoped they would in relation to the analysis questions and were able to recall the names of each of the characters so far, and their relationships with one another, so I feel they are well equipped to move on in the novel and read the remainder of the chapter tomorrow.

$\underline{P}$	**Planning** for next lesson: use bullet points

- ◆ I plan to have students continue reading and listening to Chapter 1 of the novel next class, taking guided notes in their notebooks that will help them respond to the analysis questions assignment that I'm giving them over the whole of Chapter 1: pages 1–30. This is informed from today's lesson because they did well, so we're going to continue with this method for now.

Challenges: What challenges did you encounter while working with your students?

Because it's first period and I have a quieter group, I'm getting participation from almost all students but still only hearing from a few as part of discussion.

Further Learning: What else do you need to know how to do?

If I can get white boards in time, I might try to use them for some character discussion next week to see how it goes as an alternative way to "hear" from more students.

Source: Weaver, J. C., Hartzog, M., Murnen, T., & Bertelsen, C. D. (2019). Bowling Green State University.

7.3b				
Evaluation of Instruction (SOAP)	By:		Date:	

_S_	**Subjective**: students' willingness to participate, demeanor, body language, attitude. Teacher's perceptions and reflections

Today was an independent work day. Upon glancing around the room, all students had their novels out in front of them and most had their computers open working. I did not get any questions when initially introducing the assignment, but I did have approximately five students come to my desk to ask for help with ensuring they were interpreting certain parts of the chapter correctly, or with help finding specific textual evidence to support their claims. The majority of the students seemed willing to use their class time productively and be sure they completed the assignment according to expectations.

_O_	**Observation** of student learning: anecdotal notes

Upon checking during the period after the students left, only 11/23 students had submitted their questions.

_A_	**Assessing** student learning: progress monitoring, running records, oral or written comprehension

Upon reading through the 11 responses that were submitted so far, only 1/11 students failed to include textual evidence to support their responses. The rest seem to have adequately supported their answers to analysis questions with direct evidence from the novel, which is what I was assessing today.

_P_	**Planning** for next lesson: use bullet points

- ◆ I still feel like we need to discuss the students' answers and talk about a few aspects of Chapter 1 that I didn't necessarily ask about in the reading questions, so since I don't have white boards yet, but would like to hear from more than just a few students, I'm going to try a graffiti wall activity tomorrow.

Challenges: What challenges did you encounter while working with your students?

It's difficult to assess their understanding or progress when they are each working individually at their own pace.

Further Learning: What else do you need to know how to do?

Figure out the pacing of the unit since we're moving a little slow through the novel at this point.

Source: Weaver, J. C., Hartzog, M., Murnen, T., & Bertelsen, C. D. (2019). Bowling Green State University.

The graffiti wall lesson involved students making a list of character traits for each character in the novel and listing them under that character's name on a sheet of notebook paper. Then, when students felt ready, they could come up and write the traits under each character's name on the white board to share with all of their classmates. Students could repeat traits if they wanted, since the goal was to have as much content on the board as possible for us to use to discuss their thoughts on each character. This activity allowed students more time to think through their responses than they would have had if I simply posed a question to the group and asked for their immediate thoughts through sharing verbally. This also gave them a chance to write their ideas and not have to speak their thoughts out loud in front of the entire group at once. Table 7.4 exhibits my *SOAP Notes* entry for the outcomes of the graffiti wall.

TABLE 7.4 *SOAP Notes*: Observation.

Evaluation of Instruction (SOAP)	By:		Date:	
S **Subjective**: students' willingness to participate, demeanor, body language, attitude. Teacher's perceptions and reflections				
Students collaborated for the first time this year and were even joking around a bit. They seemed engaged in the activity and about three students even got up multiple times to continue writing answers on the board. Overall, the students seemed to have a positive attitude related to the activity. I think in total, six or seven students came up to the board to write answers, which is still not the ideal amount, but more than usually participate when we just discuss aloud. At least one or two more added answers as I went over the finalized lists at the end. Students who did not get up and write words were copying the traits in their notebooks to refer to, which was still engagement. I think the students behaved positively because it was a way for them to participate without having to share aloud in front of the whole class, and it was a chance to get up and moving.				
O **Observation** of student learning: anecdotal notes				
I think the students took a lot away from the lesson because it pushed them to think and re-read to find specific details. At first, we had students participating by writing a few general words, but there were a couple characters for which I told the students that there was more information that would lead to more characteristics about that character that I wanted them to look for. In response to that, they did go back and look through the book to find more traits. One student even pointed out that I did not include Kayla as part of the character list, and when I added her, the students pointed out some important characteristics that I hadn't yet considered. I think this gave me a little more confidence about the students' willingness to dig deeper or be more thorough, and I feel like I can continue to control that by asking them to do so, since it went well today.				

(Continued)

TABLE 7.4 (Continued)

_A_	**Assessing** student learning: progress monitoring, running records, oral or written comprehension

Students were able to identify at least three traits for all nine characters listed on the board just based on evidence from Chapter 1. In most cases, students identified more than three traits. I told them they could focus on character relationships, personality traits, and physical traits, and they included a mix of all of those. They were using direct evidence from the text, often for physical descriptions, and the personality traits they developed were added to the more they discussed each character. Students exceeded expectations based on assessment of their oral and written analysis of the characters (words they wrote and a brief discussion about them as we reviewed each word). I think allowing students to write their answers instead of speak them out loud did yield more participation and helped me better assess their knowledge. Also, allowing them to collaborate. I will keep this in mind for future assessments.

_P_	**Planning** for next lesson: use bullet points

  ◆ We are going to listen to Chapter 2 and take notes. That worked well for answering the Chapter 2 analysis questions.
  ◆ We are going to be sure to address Parchman before we move on because we did not talk about it but it was featured in Chapter 1 and is important for the future of the novel.

Challenges: What challenges did you encounter while working with your students?

Some students ran out of time to copy down all of the terms. I plan to type it up for them into a chart that we can add to throughout the novel.

Further Learning: What else do you need to know how to do?

Figure out how to present the use of the N word in Chapter 2.

Source: Weaver, J. C., Hartzog, M., Murnen, T., & Bertelsen, C. D. (2019). Bowling Green State University.

Success! I realized that making a small change to *how* I was asking the students to present their thoughts and ideas significantly improved the level of participation that I saw from them beyond just reading and taking the notes. When they were given more time to think about their thoughts and ideas, and when they were not put on the spot to answer out loud in front of the whole group, they were eager to share their thoughts, and they came up with a really strong list of character traits considering they had only read the very beginning of the novel at this point.

Beyond their answers being strong and the increase in participation, I sensed some excitement among my students during this lesson because they were given an opportunity to share their ideas in a format that was comfortable for them. We added to this character list as we moved through the novel unit, and we used a similar approach to this when we discussed motifs throughout the novel. Participation continued to be higher than I'd seen before, all thanks to this small change because of a pattern I noticed in my *SOAP Notes* reflections.

Additionally, toward the end of my three weeks of reflections, I started to realize that although I'd made a change that increased participation during our discussions of major characters and motifs in the novel, much of our class time was still spent preparing the students for larger discussions, and that involved the audiobook and notes, without much talking in between. As a result, I began to feel that I wasn't doing enough actual "teaching."

Normally when teaching a novel, I'd read aloud with the students or offer them more specified guided reading opportunities on their own and we'd at least talk a little bit about what they'd read, rather than them just using the Canvas discussion boards to do so. It felt weird to go whole class periods without much noise aside from the audiobook. This left me feeling like I wasn't interacting with my students enough and was doing them a disservice.

Once again, I realized I needed to change my mindset on how I approached reviewing my *SOAP Notes* reflections, and what I realized was that for the second time, I was making assumptions about what the students wanted or needed without actually communicating with them. I want my lessons to be student-centered. I was teaching seniors who were going to need to know in the very near future how to monitor their own learning and what worked for them. Through this thought process, I realized that if I wanted to really know how engaged students were in the lessons when we weren't discussing, I should just *ask* my students! And that is exactly what I did. I administered a survey to students asking them questions about their level of engagement in the lessons and their understanding of the novel (see Table 7.5).

TABLE 7.5 Teacher/Student Feedback

Please answer the questions below to provide Ms. Chavez with some feedback about the unit and the novel so far.

1. What do you think of the novel? Is it engaging? Is it relatable? Why or why not?
2. How are the methods we've been using working out?
    a. Is the audiobook working well for the reading? Would you prefer some days to be able to read to yourself instead?
    b. I've noticed less and less people taking notes. Be honest: Is this because you're just feeling lazy first period, or are the notes not helpful? Is there a different way we should approach taking notes over the chapter? Some of you have expressed the notes ARE helpful. If notes are not helpful, would pausing to check in and discuss throughout the chapter work better?
    c. Are there any other types of lessons you'd like to try to engage more with the book? EX: journaling, formal discussions, more written assignments, etc.
    d. Are you content with how we are already doing things: read, take notes, and answer questions and online discussion. Keep it simple. If so, let me know that, too!
3. (Optional) Any other thoughts on the unit so far or ideas for future chapters or future years of teaching the novel in senior English:

I wasn't sure what to expect from students, but their responses were largely positive. Of the 15 students present that day who completed the survey, all 15 stated that they were content with how the unit had already progressed and felt like they were learning and keeping up well with the lessons. 13/15 stated they'd prefer continuing to use the audiobook as well, and that it helped them understand what they were reading.

Reflecting on their feedback, I consider this survey to be the most valuable implementation from my *SOAP Notes* and daily reflective practice. I don't think, having not been encouraged to closely examine students' engagement and my lesson design on a daily basis, I would have taken the time to ask my students for their thoughts and feedback—and that made all the difference. Not only did I learn a lot about how students were engaging with the novel unit and what I could change to help them improve, but the feedback from students helped me build trust and continue more confidently as their teacher the rest of the year.

I have made this practice of checking in with students a permanent part of each unit I teach, and it has continued to provide me with valuable information about how lessons are going, and what I can change to better meet the students' needs because *they're* the ones sharing with me. Since finishing the novel unit, I taught a research essay unit and a play in this class. During each of these units, I surveyed students about their engagement and progress based on what I sensed, and each time, I was able to use their feedback to guide my instruction to increase participation or better meet their needs in some way. I've also used this in my other classes, surveying my students about their reading preferences to help design my approach for teaching novels.

An added benefit of keeping up with this practice is building trust with my students. An unexpected benefit is that it has helped me trust myself more. This is the note I'd like to end on. Did my daily *SOAP Notes* and reflecting on my lessons help me improve my instruction in the obvious ways of implementing new approaches specific to my students' needs? Absolutely! Do I think that it helped me improve trust and relationships between my students and me? For sure! But something truly invaluable I took away from this practice that I wasn't expecting was validation. I should admit that when I initially began completing my daily reflections, I *was* finding myself falling into the trap of only using them to criticize myself and found myself feeling a bit down for not working hard enough to prepare more engaging lessons for my students.

It was when I reframed my mindset and approach to these lesson reflections that I started to realize everything I *was* already doing. I could have taken the deficit approach of telling myself that I shouldn't have missed such an obvious solution when working with a quiet group of students as using white boards and graffiti walls so they could write their answers instead of speaking them. I could have told myself I'm an ineffective teacher for not noticing this need earlier and starting the unit with such an approach. I could feel regret for not including a survey to collect student feedback in my first unit of the year, since that's something we're taught to do in our teacher training, and I should have known. But how would that help me improve?

Changing my mindset helped establish the ways in which my lessons improved as a result of my *SOAP Notes.*

I discovered through reflecting with *SOAP Notes* and checking in with my students that I don't have to do it all in one lesson, one week, or even one unit. Sometimes less is more, and sometimes keeping it simple can be exactly what the students, and you, need. The majority of my students were enjoying the novel and the opportunity to quietly reflect on what they were reading, and I was the one creating a problem where there wasn't one. As one of my students put it, "If it's not broken, don't fix it."

Since then, I have been able to approach my lessons more confidently because I'm able to trust that much of what I'm doing is working, and that has improved the classes in unexpected ways. Sure, as a result of practicing daily reflections, my students are participating more in the lessons—an important achievement. Moreover, as a result of practicing daily reflection through *SOAP Notes*, I'm also seeing students ask for help more often, I'm seeing them feel more comfortable communicating their needs, I'm noticing I do a better job of modeling the importance and excitement of the content I'm teaching, students and I are building closer relationships, and I'm looking forward to coming to work now more than I ever have before.

TAKE-AWAYS

SOAP Notes **reflective practice can develop:**

- ◆ A more student-centered classroom
- ◆ Student voice
- ◆ Student-led learning with student assessment
- ◆ Develop active student participation
- ◆ Monitoring of their own learning
- ◆ Student–teacher relationships and trust
- ◆ Teacher confidence

8

Gifted, Talented, Exceptional, and Still Working on It

Anna Wank

GETTING TO KNOW THE AUTHOR

♦ Middle school English teacher
♦ 4th year of teaching
♦ Suburban school system

My student population is incredibly unique. Unlike most of the other teachers in my school, I have an opportunity to teach them my subject in each of the three grades that they will go through at my school. That is, every day of their 6th, 7th, and 8th grade lives, I get to have them in my class for reading and language arts instruction that stretches beyond the traditional classroom. Students can be designated as gifted in many different areas to qualify for the program, including *superior cognitive ability, creative thinking ability, specific academic ability* (in any of their core subjects), or *visual and performing arts ability* (in subjects such as drama, dance, music, or visual arts). The vast majority of my students qualify in several of these various areas.

DOI: 10.4324/9781003493464-13

The idea of describing gifted and talented students in one lump sum is, in itself, impossible to do. While there are definitely trends and typical behaviors or interests in my students, they are, by definition, quite exceptional. One of the goals that I have placed priority on within my classroom is forming a strong rapport with my students and encouraging them to feel comfortable with their peers in an effort to create a sort of educational "family"—after all, the majority of these students have been and will continue to be in the same courses throughout their local schooling. Providing a safe space for my students to learn and test out new activities (and to occasionally fail in them—a concept that is incredibly foreign to many a gifted student) is invaluable to their understanding and appreciation of the educational process.

My Curriculum

In my program, we (the other professionals who are involved in the program) currently have a multitude of resources that we use to assist our students. Generally, the planning is broken down into two sections—Reading and Language Arts. In Reading, we incorporate both selections from our textbook offerings as well as many additional books that correspond to the learning standards. In the lesson that is reflected upon below using *SOAP Notes*, the text that my 7th grade class was working through was *The Outsiders* by S. E. Hinton.

How Did Reflective Practice Impact My Instruction?

During a process of 15 days, I took *SOAP Notes* regarding each of my lessons as they were happening. These notes assisted me throughout the 15 days by reinvigorating my reflection process during the lessons and helped me to make more positive changes in my classroom during the short span of time that they were recorded. Each of the categories listed in the following sections are areas that I was able to concentrate and improve on during instruction.

Grouping

While reflecting on the lessons involved in my *SOAP* noting process, I noticed that during the first week, a vast majority of the activities I had planned for students were designed for them to complete individually. However, when I reflect on the level of student engagement, it is nearly always higher when students are able to work in groups with each other. According to Matthews and Dai (2014), "Best practice involves grouping students for advanced curriculum work in flexibly organized ways that are matches to documented learning needs, which can happen in a number of different ways" (p. 347). In a classroom such as mine, with many students who have individual social and learning needs, an increase in classroom time spent in groups proved to be beneficial in several ways, including (but not limited to) student involvement, idea sharing, creativity, and meeting our daily standards.

Grouping situations varied from assigned pairs to large chosen peer groups and more. Based on my reflection in *SOAP Notes*, I found that the most productive groupings for strictly outlined activities were those who were grouped with similar learning needs and abilities, while the most effective grouping for creativity proved to be larger and involve many different types of students. "A creative discovery is not usually the product of an individual mind; it is more frequently the product of synergistic interaction, involving a group of people, none of whom are likely to make the same discovery of their own" (Matthews & Dai, 2014, p. 337). This was particularly noticeable in activities such as the weekly journal prompt, where students were able to share the many different directions that they chose to go with each prompt. After writing, students were able to share with a group, and then give each of their peers some verbal feedback on their responses.

Student Investment

As discussed previously, the level of work that is involved in the gifted programming at my district is intensive and complex. While many people may assume that all gifted students automatically have a great deal of investment in their own learning, this is not necessarily the case. Yes, there are plenty of students who are very invested, but as the teacher in a gifted classroom, I found that in my reflective *SOAP Notes*, I was not drawing attention to the level of commitment those students show. "The pleasure that children and adolescents take in the learning process is critical to their eventual cognitive and academic outcomes, and an intense desire to take learning as far as possible is essential to extraordinary accomplishment" (Matthews & Dai, 2014, p. 346). In an effort to recognize and praise high levels of student investment, I chose to gradually ingratiate verbal praise to those students who showed great initiative, as well as complete some other types of communication with students who did not show that they were particularly invested in their education.

One of the most effective types of communication I had with students who were on the lower end of the spectrum was engaging in one-on-one meetings. For example, during this time I had one particular student who was having difficulty completing his day-to-day work and was becoming quite frustrated with the class. In addition to contacting his parents on a regular basis, I chose, during these 15 days of *SOAP* noting, to pull the student aside during some of the more student-centered activities in order to talk about what would be needed from him. For the most part, I found that these conversations became easier and more student-led over time—questions I asked such as, "What assignments do we know are missing?" turned into much more involved questions, such as, "Where would be the best resource to look for help on our Grammar Page homework?" or "What are the best methods for studying your weekly stems?"

Even throughout the short three weeks of note-taking, I could see that the student was taking ownership of his education to a higher degree and becoming more confident in class. This was made evident by not only his rising weekly test scores but also his participation in daily discussions and contributions of ideas.

Creativity

At the heart of the middle school gifted language arts and reading curriculum, there is creativity—one of the reasons that

I became a teacher, and one of the best things I remember from going through school myself. It is one of the most centralized tenants in gifted education—and yet, upon *SOAP Notes* reflection, I felt that creativity in the classroom could be expanded. According to Abdulla Alabbasi et al. (2021), "As for educational programs, gifted students benefit greatly from learning strategies and tactics that target creative thinking skills. This can be accomplished in many ways, some of which involve infusing originality and other creative thinking skills into the curriculum" (p. 399). I found that, perhaps, in class, we had traded some of the adventure of creativity for the comfort of routine.

I began to think of ways to incorporate creativity into some of our more rigid activities. What would our grammar lessons be like if I were to allow students to finish sentences however they would like? Would they show a higher level of interest, or even comprehension, when practicing with their own creative and silly sentences rather than examples from a text? In my class, as it turns out, the answer was a resounding yes! While it is not always simple to implement creativity into every lesson, I have made it a priority in my lesson planning (from the beginning of the *SOAP Notes* reflection process onward) to allow for more open-ended participation and creativity from students to find its way between the lectures, studying, and behavior management.

How Did *SOAP Notes* Reflective Practice Impact My Own Learning About My Instruction?

After the process of *SOAP Notes* reflection took place, I found that I still had several questions about how to make my classes even more interesting and effective for students. As this is my first year teaching specifically gifted classes, I know that I had to do some deep digging research to find out what others in the field thought. Subsequently, I list several of the most pertinent topics that I was able to research and hope to further incorporate into my classes.

Motivation

My classes, like all classes, can occasionally go through a lapse in motivation. Through reflection, I find that it is most present in our grammar activities, as well as activities that students have simply "shut themselves off from"—that is, students have determined that they are not good at the objective and, rather than feeling the uncomfortableness of failure, have simply decided the activity is not for them. While I believe that this partially stems from a lack of growth mindset, as discussed further in the chapter, I believe that it is critical for me to continue pushing students toward high motivation.

We (teachers and students) need to work together in the classroom to identify and nurture the environment that contributes to high motivation and recognize what sort of environments may lower motivation, and this is where *SOAP* noting was beneficial.

Growth Mindset

Similar to motivation, I hope to further instill a growth mindset in my gifted students. Many gifted students, at some point, go through the same cycle; they are deemed as gifted, they feel great about learning, they confront something that is difficult (which they are not used to—after all, they're supposed to be smart, right?), they become frustrated because learning has almost always come naturally, and they then get discouraged by the idea of failing. I believe that a great deal of this can be chalked up to a lack of instilling a growth mindset in students.

Through the process of writing *SOAP Notes*, reflecting on them, and doing further research into the field of best practices in gifted and talented education, I have learned a great deal and have widened the overall scope of what I want my classroom to be. From more simple daily changes to bigger concepts that should be addressed during curriculum design, I now have a functional list of tasks and priorities going into the next year of my career.

When we think of the potential futures that any of our students are capable of, the limits truly are endless. In order to be a helpful stepping stone along the way, it is vital to not only stop to take note of your instructional strategies but also to engage in continual reflective practice, possibly using *SOAP Notes*, to focus on student learning.

TAKE-AWAYS

SOAP Notes **reflective practice can develop:**

♦ Grouping for instruction
♦ Student investment in learning
♦ Instructional decision-making
♦ Student inquiry and creativity
♦ Student motivation
♦ Teacher inquiry and research

References

Abdulla Alabbasi, A. M., Hafsyan, A. S. M., Runco, M. A., & AlSaleh, A. (2021). Problem finding, divergent thinking, and evaluative thinking among gifted and nongifted students. *Journal for the Education of the Gifted*, *44*(4), 398–413. https://doi.org/10.1177/01623532211044539

Matthews, D. J., & Dai, D.Y. (2014). Gifted education: Changing conceptions, emphases and practice. *International Studies in Sociology of Education*, *24*(4), 335–353. https://doi.org/10.1080/09620214.2014.979578

Part III

Deep Dive into Instruction and Learning via Reflective *SOAP Notes*

Teachers' Perceptions
of Instruction

9

The Lord of the Flies, The Boys and Their Beast, and Me with My Notes

Erin Dziak

GETTING TO KNOW THE AUTHOR

- ♦ Middle school English teacher
- ♦ 2nd year of teaching
- ♦ Urban, parochial school

Introduction and Demographics

My *SOAP Notes* were taken in my 7th grade class, a class that started off the year with several behavioral and bullying problems. Our middle school team has had multiple parent meetings and incredible help from our administration. At the time of my *SOAP Notes*, our 7th graders seemed to have turned a corner and were ready to fully engage in our lessons. The 7th graders were reading pages 48–144 in *The Lord of the Flies* that led up to the mid-novel assessment.

DOI: 10.4324/9781003493464-16

The current 7th grade class was mostly fully remote last year because of *COVID-19*; therefore, the students have needed a transitional time to come back to the classroom and become acclimated and fully engaged. This has led to some behavioral concerns as well as areas for academic improvement. When I was able to understand what was specifically causing certain behaviors in my classroom, I was more aware of how to address them and ask for advice when needed. I mentioned in my *SOAP Notes*, "I saw a lot of students stay quiet and pay attention, but there were times closer to the end of the period where they were asleep or zoning out." This is a behavior that I have seen a lot throughout my time with this class. The 7th grade class is right after lunch from 1:20 to 3:00. Students are often tired and only have my class and religion left before the end of the day.

I have struggled with effective strategies to keep the students awake and engaged after lunch. But with the *SOAP Notes*, I was more aware of my students and able to reflect on the problem and asked my principal for more strategies to use. For example, I was able to make this note, "NOT A STUDENT FELL ASLEEP TODAY! Big day! One student did ask twice if he could fall asleep, but he stayed awake when I told him no. He was cold called a couple times to stay alert." When students are awake and actively working in their books, we have made incredible progress. Since *SOAP Notes*, we have implemented more annotation in books (students get to keep their novels at the end of the unit) and what-to-do directions to keep students ready and accountable for their learning.

Just like the boy in *The Lord of the Flies* who had to confront the fact that the Beast they had been chasing around was them the entire time, I had to re-examine my own teaching and classroom culture multiple times throughout the school year. I continued to see growth in my own writings, but looking retrospectively at my *SOAP Notes*, I was able to see growth in my own teaching and mental health. This year was one of ups and downs. Some days I felt like Ralph when he first crash-landed on the island, bright-eyed and ready to take on the world, and other days I felt like Ralph at the very end of the novel, dirty and panting with the island completely on fire.

Throughout my *SOAP Notes*, I was able to continue to see trends in my writings and problems in my classroom that needed to be solved. For example, I wrote, "I was excited because this was an exciting part of the book and one that I previewed yesterday. It was quiet when [students] walked into the room and it was peaceful. The students were focused on their book . . ."

How *SOAP Notes* Impacted Student Learning Based on Reflection

Again, I saw learning happening during the mid-novel assessment for *Lord of the Flies*. I noted, "I had to take a moment and stop helping people on the test because I was so taken by how he remembered, internalized, and applied this knowledge" when a student was able to take out a small excerpt from a lesson that I taught about philosophy. The day we talked about the philosophers was the day that I mentioned previously, when not a single student fell asleep. After grading the tests, I found that the student wasn't the only one who understood that question. Another example from my *SOAP Notes* was when I stated, "we didn't have any new pages to read today so they didn't have a lull period that typically catches some of them." This note allows me to see that the students were able to utilize instructional time, had a high participation ratio, and were able to retain that information.

The Challenges of *SOAP Notes*

One of the challenges I faced in creating my *SOAP Notes* was finding the time to write down meaningful data. I chose a class that was followed up by my planning period, but I was not always able to use that time to write my notes. I found that my *SOAP Notes* were lacking without the appropriate time given. Reflection is a skill that requires practice, and if *SOAP Notes* and reflective teaching are to continue in the classroom, there would need to be a consistent effort to have meaningful connections and understandings about the concerns or areas of growth in my classroom. I know that *SOAP Notes* are able to work with a teacher's schedule and can be used in the moment or after the fact, but I found it difficult to find an appropriate time to write out my notes to make sure that they were accurate. Again, this can stem from a lack of practice with the technique and a natural, reflective rhythm can emerge with consistent habits.

The Benefits of *SOAP Notes*

As a new teacher, I am always trying to discover new ways to adapt my teaching style and better my practice. I have taught the 7th grade curriculum in my previous school year and was able to teach it multiple times a day. This year, with a change in class structure and 8th grade curriculum, I was only teaching the 7th grade curriculum to one class. Throughout my *SOAP Notes*, I was able to reflect on my teaching and how my instruction was changing from day to day.

In the *Observation* section of my *SOAP Notes*, I stated, "[s]tudents are awake during class, but they aren't necessarily engaged. I need to figure out a good way in order to make sure that students aren't distracted during class." While this observation and reflection doesn't give any action steps, it is the first step to brainstorming and receiving those next stages. The *SOAP Notes* allowed for a space to take a minute or two to think about what I needed from my class and instruction to improve. When approached later in the year about engagement, I was able to point out behaviors I see from my students, and it created an environment where other master teachers were able to offer advice to me.

SOAP Notes also offered me a view into successes in my classroom that I forgot about. Teaching can sometimes feel like the entire world is imploding in a single second and then the sun is shining a moment later. For example, I wrote about a student who was able to remember a detail about three different philosophers from one lesson and apply that knowledge on his test. This was a small moment, but at the time, it meant everything to me. During this period of time, our school, especially our middle school, was in the middle of a "culture crisis." We were in panic mode, trying to address and fix any problems we had with our instruction, organization, and classroom management. It was important for me to be able to see the little joys that continued to happen throughout this time period. *SOAP Notes* acted as a way for me to reflect on my classroom management and instruction, but it also made it possible for me to celebrate these small moments of joy as well.

Takeaways

The *SOAP Notes* technique offers educators an informative and reflective way to continue to imagine their own classroom. I found that it made concerns more tangible, and I was able to focus on and voice my concerns after being slightly removed from the class. The technique also makes it possible to continue to work on and practice reflection in the classroom. With consistency, this technique is able to open up multiple avenues of teacher preparation and advancement.

While there were days when I felt like Ralph running through the forest, trying to escape his certain doom, I know that there were also days when I wasn't. Teaching is cyclical and can bring on really important discussions while also bringing in days when the hours seem to drag on for a week. The *SOAP Notes* model allowed me to reflect on both of these days to see what went right, but more importantly, to find solutions, revisions, and modifications to strengthen student learning and instruction.

TAKE-AWAYS

SOAP Notes **reflective practice helped:**

- Imagine an improved classroom
- Elevate student successes
- With brainstorming and next steps
- Manage time
- Identify effective classroom management strategies

10

Fluidity and Flexibility in Honors Courses

Gabrielle Day

GETTING TO KNOW THE AUTHOR

- Middle school English teacher
- 3rd year of teaching
- Private parochial school

I've taught Honors Language Arts, but a challenge I was currently facing in my new school was the fact that my students were not in fact honors students. In stark contrast to my previous honors classes, filled with students who exceeded the basic expectations of a traditional course but who needed just as much guidance and support with critical thinking as their "traditional" peers, this class was absorbing content in minutes and then playing on their chromebooks for the second half of class. After about three class periods, I knew that even though I finally received my wish to have a class filled with strong critical thinkers, it was clear that I needed to find a better way to meet their needs for rigorous, purposeful learning. They were really nice kids who

DOI: 10.4324/9781003493464-17

worked beyond the expectations of a regular class, but these students were not yet prepared for the rigor of an honors class.

I started using the time we had left over as discussion to get more information about what they wanted to learn and what interested them. The unit detailed in my *SOAP Notes* is one that began as construction of choice in the classroom derived from our early conversations. I allowed students in the class to submit and then vote on nonfiction topics of interest. The highest number of consistent votes was for conspiracy theories, but I wanted a more concrete path, so when I saw a trend of "the Salem witch trials," I knew I could incorporate their beloved conspiracy theories into our learning. They unanimously agreed this was the way they wanted to go with their next unit. We would focus on the impact of mass hysteria on history, and we would use *The Crucible* by Arthur Miller as our anchor text.

SOAPing Up *The Crucible*

I knew this unit would make an interesting unit for my *SOAP Notes* reflection because of the reflective component that I could utilize to assess and modify the ins and outs of this challenging unit. Typically taught in 11th grade, *The Crucible* was a huge gamble for us to take in terms of vocabulary and content, but I knew if I could get them interested right off the bat then they would be more committed to the story. I began with *Sinners in the Hands of an Angry God* to set the tone of our novel, hoping that the tone and unreasonable expectations of Puritan life might peak their interest, but it backfired. I noted that the students were painfully bored and also beyond uncomfortable at the idea that this was the beginning of the unit. The wording was too hard, and the length made them (and myself) nervous that they had chosen wrong. I could see through my *SOAP* noting the instant regret on their faces. It took a lot of convincing and encouragement that our whole unit would not in fact be me screaming at them about "hellfire and brimstone," though that was a large part of the Puritanical religion, and I vowed that the next piece would be more interesting, still hoping to keep their buy-in long enough to prove what they had chosen was worth it.

I reflected that night on the best way to divide students into different groups with unique research. I asked for ideas and resources from my 11th grade English teacher. I used a modified version of her original project that helped establish background information about key themes and information students would grapple with during reading. Groups were broken down into different topics. Students had three class periods to answer a series of topic specific questions and view provided research before presenting to the class. I facilitated discussions within the small groups and answered questions on vocabulary that was challenging or helped students make connections. If the group projects were successful and the students could manage the pre-reading work with limited difficulty, then I knew we could safely conquer the play even if vocabulary posed a challenge. Our three-day project took longer, and I noted this with mild disappointment in my *SOAP Notes*, but by the end of presentations, I was confident that we were ready.

The groups had taken their pre-reading presentations seriously and drew connections that I had not made previously. I could not control my excitement at their engagement levels during presentations and the thoughtful questions that came from their work. My *SOAP Notes* focused on how we could keep this level of engagement as we moved from presentations to the book. As much as I adore and believe in *The Crucible*, there is no mistaking the heaviness of the book, and even with all the surprising engagement, I was consistently worried if I had put too much stock into a book I hadn't read since high school. I swallowed my worries and charged forward and doled out parts.

At the end of Act I, I had them make inferences about the rest of the text. I really wanted to see how students were feeling. I noted in my Day 6 *SOAP Notes* that I would ask them how they came to their inferences before we resumed the play the next day. The Day 7 *SOAP Notes* recorded that we began discussing how students arrived at their inferences from the previous class. I noted that I would take more time with this assignment if given the opportunity because students needed to support their inferences, but we didn't have time. This revision would bring the question to the higher level of depth of knowledge (DOK) that is expected in an honors class. Students claimed a variety of reasons for their answers, but I think it is pertinent to note that the majority of the students rationalized that their answers were based around the context clues, background information on the Salem witch trials, and the research we had done on Arthur Miller. They knew this was an allegory for the Red Scare and that historically many accused did not make it out.

The physical reading of *The Crucible* took us about a week. My *SOAP Notes* during this time noted the difficulty of the vocabulary but the high endurance of my students. I paused frequently during the reading of stage directions and stopped students if I noticed them struggling with a word or set of words. The *SOAP Notes* helped me prepare a few solid questions I knew would need to be discussed at some point during each lecture, but I still left the timing flexible.

Because of my *SOAP Notes*, I was reminded that the students were indifferent to the fact John Proctor had given the Salem trial the "ultimate finger," as they labeled it, because he had elected to be hung rather than sign a document lying about his involvement in witchcraft. I figured that was it, and I had just wasted the last two weeks of my life—but they weren't emotionless; they were just angry, and this was evident during our discussions of the book. I wrote in my *SOAP Notes* that we watched the movie the next two class periods and compared and contrasted the characters, and the students were pleased with the portrayals of John Proctor and Abigail, but being confronted with the film version of Tituba made them uncomfortable. I further noted that we had discussed her being a slave from Barbados, but several expressed that they weren't even sure where that was.

The final assessment for this project was a project on mass hysteria. Students needed to come up with any historical event that affected large quantities of people and connect it back to *The Crucible* and the insanity of mass hysteria. Students were able to work together in a team of two or on their own. We brainstormed as a class briefly, and students were given a list of preselected topics with the idea that they were allowed to pick a different topic if it gained their interest.

The students spent several days conducting research to help with their assignment. They created a slides project that gave a historical context, and the effect of the hysteria on our culture and the future, and were able to provide parallels between their event and *The Crucible*. They then completed a metacognitive conference with me where they discussed the strengths and weaknesses of the unit and their project. Based on my *SOAP Notes* reflection, the student reviews of the project were overwhelmingly positive and the meetings were useful.

SOAP Notes were a benefit to this unit because I was able to record and revise with a simple, followable, template. I found that I was not only able to track my students and assess comprehension, critical thinking skills, and engagement, but also inform and modify my own instruction and my ability to plan a unit with choice at the center. I took a big risk with a huge group of incredibly bright students. I wanted my students to have choice, and it paid off, thanks largely-in-part, to my *SOAP note* records.

TAKE-AWAYS

SOAP Notes **reflective practice helped:**

- ◆ Imagine the power of student choice
- ◆ Build instructional confidence
- ◆ Design and reflect on curriculum
- ◆ Construct strategies for student success
- ◆ Elevate student learning through critical thinking

Building Student–Teacher Relationships

11

My *SOAP Notes* Journey through Nonverbal Communication

Amy Farrar

GETTING TO KNOW THE AUTHOR

♦ High school English teacher
♦ 34th year of teaching
♦ Suburban school

Throughout my teaching journey, I have been intrigued with—okay, perhaps a pedagogy geek about—the craft of teaching: direct instruction, differentiated instruction, immediate feedback, and reflection, to name a few. As an ardent practitioner of direct instruction, I wondered: What if *SOAP Notes* could help me learn to model the nonverbal indicators I sought for my students to use to indicate their level of mastery of a particular standard or concept I was teaching? How much would their nonverbal behavior enable me to understand who needed differentiated instruction—whether remediation or enrichment? What if my students' immediate nonverbal communication

DOI: 10.4324/9781003493464-19

could tip off their level of learning more expediently but still as accurately as formative assessment? Foremost, would the opportunity to reflect on *SOAP Notes* catalyze higher levels of student performance? This *SOAP Notes* experience enabled me to hone my observation skills, focusing just as much on what my students did (actions, eye contact, facial expressions, gestures, body positions) as what they said, thus adding significant feedback to inform my teaching practices.

SOAP Notes in an English Classroom

As an English teacher, my students and I discuss the fifth wall—the reader who is listening and observing the characters in the room in the literary work. The reader observes all the characters say and do as well as all they don't say and don't do—otherwise known as nonverbal communication. This outsider perspective tends to be less biased, thus more credible. *SOAP Notes* cast *me* as the fifth wall, observing and analyzing my students. It created a less-biased lens from which I could more objectively observe the interactions among the characters in the room: students and teacher (me!).

Furthermore, as an English teacher, I was especially intrigued by the *SOAP Notes* nonverbal communication focus because listening and speaking is one of the state of Ohio's six English Language Arts (ELA) learning strands (Ohio Department of Education, 2022). This *SOAP Notes* experience spotlights listening and speaking, ubiquitous in an ELA classroom lush with literary analysis. Therefore, my *SOAP Notes* journey taught me to more adeptly assess this standard by focusing on what students did as they listened and to see its connection to academic performance.

The *SOAP Notes* quantitative practice of observing specific behaviors enabled me to see a preponderance of large and small head nods as I taught the lesson. During our class discussions about the novella *The Awakening*, I noted that students who participated more verbally and those who used large or small head nods whether the teacher or a student was explaining an interpretation scored higher on the first short-term summative assessment/quiz. Notwithstanding two outliers, students with more rigid body positions and flatter facial expressions did not score in the top percentile.

These *SOAP* outcomes had me question other ways their nonverbal communication was coding their skill levels before they spoke or after I spoke. Could I *see* their understanding or confusion before I heard it, before I assessed? Further *SOAP Notes* indicated that I could. Tilted head, pursed lips, and averted eyes also seemed to indicate less understanding. But now, prior to the second quiz, having been informed via the nonverbal communication of the students who needed additional help, I could improve my instruction practices. I paired students with nonverbal behaviors that indicated less understanding with those whose nonverbal communication indicated more understanding. I then posed further, same-standard literary discussion questions for these small groups.

I stopped at each group to overhear their discussion, especially listening to and observing the respective verbal and nonverbal communication of the students whose prior nonverbal communication during the whole class discussion indicated less understanding. If their verbal comments validated their lack of understanding, I stopped to have a one-on-one conversation to clarify meaning, discuss textual evidence, and drag out their commentary (explanations and rationales) to further their understanding. These *SOAP Notes*–informed practices of student modeling and individual instruction perhaps contributed to the raised scores on the next quiz: The average score on the first *The Awakening* quiz was 82.6 percent, but on the second quiz was 87.1 percent. Needless to say, I was a quick convert to continue the less-biased observation process, analysis, and reflection of the practice of *SOAP Notes*.

Early on, *SOAP Notes* prodded two epiphanies for me, one I had immediately and the other I had over the course of a few weeks of using *SOAP Notes*, but both informed and improved my teaching practices. More immediately, based on the previously mentioned nonverbal communication skills indicating student lack of understanding, I provided instant, specific student- or teacher-modeling of the desired skill and provided further imme-diate practice in the classroom at the point of instruction when student nonverbal behavior indicated a lack of understanding. I felt confident making these lesson plan changes the moment I saw them, believing they would foster student growth and learning.

However, the other epiphany did not come until after the cumulative nature of taking *SOAP Notes* for several weeks enabled me to see patterns of behavior that highlighted further nonverbal behaviors that indicated either the presence or lack of students' understanding. In fact, it took the use of *SOAP Notes* during mask-wearing to reveal these patterns.

Can Nonverbal Communication Be Masked?

Mask-Wearing Effects on Nonverbal Communication

Before revealing my epiphany, it is notable how mask-wearing affected *SOAP Notes*. When mask mandates were upon virtu-ally all of us, I immediately abandoned taking *SOAP Notes* on nonverbal communication, hoping to resume it whenever the mandate ended, for how could I effectively evaluate nonverbal communication without seeing their whole face? Two months later, missing the feedback the practice afforded and desiring to continue my journey having learned the value and vitality of nonverbal communication, I renewed my *SOAP Notes* practice—even with masks on.

But first, I had to evaluate my students' mindset: could I even seek to use *SOAP Notes* to inform, change, and improve my instruction if students were not mentally prepared to further their learning. So, for the next week, I focused the nonverbal communication *SOAP Notes* on my perception of their social-emotional attitude and alacrity (or lack thereof) toward learning in this new mask-wearing classroom envi-ronment. My *SOAP Notes* behavior observations revealed three main student emotions as reflected by their nonverbal communication:

1. **Apathy**: no eye contact, staring straight ahead, no body movements toward speakers, no hand raising, no gestures, neutral body position, lethargy, eyebrows motionless
2. **Disconnection**: downcast or limited eye contact, limited body turn toward the speaker or toward their audience when they spoke, sagging body position, less vitality in their movements, little to no head nodding or hand raising, eyebrows furrowed
3. **Engagement**: eye contact, but rarely sustained as before mask-wearing; body movements toward the speaker or audience; erect posture; vitality in their movements; less speaking than before mask-wearing, but accompanied with more pronounced head nodding to ensure communication, eyebrows raised slightly at the ends as if indicative of a smile

During mask-wearing my *SOAP Notes* revealed this continuum of student behavior changes. They were like turning down the volume knob on the radio regardless of the current volume. Students who were "loud," enthusiastic communicators and learners became less emotional but engaged; the "medium volume," engaged students often became reserved or sad; the previous "low volume" students appeared silent and apathetic. Invariably, mask-wearing muzzled my students verbally as well as nonverbally, thus lessening my understanding of their current performance level and content understanding.

However, whether my prior *SOAP Notes* observations were oblivious or whether mask-wearing accentuated it, my new observations revealed the value of analyzing eyebrow movements. This was a form of nonverbal communication that I had not previously recognized, but now with the majority of their faces covered, it became key in identifying student learning needs. Having the opportunity to look at the cumulative nature of my *SOAP Notes* highlighted that eyebrow movements were new and frequent observations. As you may recall, the volume continuum revealed the following: seemingly apathetic students showed motionless eyebrows; sad and somewhat confused students showed furrowed eyebrows; and the most engaged and highest achieving students often raised their eyebrows slightly at the ends as if indicative of a smile.

Lessons During Mask-Wearing

Now undaunted—and inquisitive about the nonverbal behaviors masking-wearing might further bring—I prepared a character development lesson. My junior honors English students were immersed in understanding the relationships among the five main characters in Kate Chopin's novella *The Awakening*. I wanted to ensure that they noticed Chopin's craft in creating pairs of male and female foils (characters with opposite traits) who shaped the choices made by the main character in her journey to self-awakening.

I asked them a typical process question based on their understanding of the characters thus far: Did they believe doing a character web analysis would be more fruitful as a class or in small groups? I was stunned. I got zero verbal and zero nonverbal feedback—oh the masks! My students normally respond with alacrity and vitality when asked for their learning preferences.

Curious by what I'd witnessed during this mask-wearing time, I gave them a directive: "I need to *see* how you feel about doing this character web. Please *show* me how you feel about working on it together as a class." Wow! Their bodies exploded with messages. Several students gave a thumbs up then immediately sat up straight, ready to take notes on our class character web discussion. I saw four students give exaggerated head nods. I asked them, "What does this pronounced head nod mean?" They replied that they definitely wanted to discuss the connections among all of the characters. Therefore, *SOAP Notes* reflections revealed that with the mask silencing their verbal feedback, it exaggerated their nonverbal feedback.

Students "answered" with other nonverbal feedback: three students with slight hand raises, two with head tilts with slight nods, and a few others paused with no change in body positioning and no gesturing. Curious about the rationales behind the variance of their similar nonverbal responses, I directly asked students what their body language meant. The three students with slight hand raises said they wanted to discuss characterization as a class but since character webs are used as a more basic means of understanding character development, each had some uncertainty: Would class discussion reveal depth of character development? Another student worried if she would appear to her honors-level classmates to lack understanding of the novella's basics. And one apathetic student admitted he did not really care how we analyzed characterization.

The two students with head tilts and slight nods both stated that they needed a moment to think about my question before deciding if a class discussion would be more fruitful. As for those with no change in nonverbal communication, two admitted they weren't listening, one apologized that she had "zoned out," and the other stated that she was "anxiously stressing about other schoolwork she had to complete by tomorrow."

My biggest takeaway from this one question regards those who had no change in body movement when asked for nonverbal feedback because it informed me that students were off-task–not confused, not reluctant, and not unsure. As teachers, we've perhaps all witnessed the "zoned out" look. However, these students did not display that archetypal expression even though the behavior (being off-task) was the same. Perhaps students I had previously thought were apathetic or confused were really off-task and needing my redirection. In the future, I can move proximally to students who show no movement after a question, or I can re-ask the question and wait for some movement or word to guide me further in determining their understanding.

Overall, mask-wearing contributed to nonverbal communication being emphatically exaggerated so it would be noticed, or eliminated altogether unless prodded by the teacher. Regardless, both exemplify unauthentic, nontraditional nonverbal communication that can create gaps in teacher awareness of student learning and emotions. Desiring to maintain the integrity of this experience, I chose to wait until students were unmasked to continue *SOAP Notes*.

Masks Removed

It wasn't until masks were removed that I realized the type of nonverbal form of communication I missed most was the daily emotion-filled facial expressions of my students: smiles when happy and understanding; frowns when sad, intimidated, or perplexed by content; and grimaces when upset or frustrated with learning or the learning process. More specifically, I was shocked by how much I rely on a student's mouth and overall facial expression to apprise me of his or her emotions—which often indicate their level of understanding and academic engagement—yet I realized that although mask-wearing may muffle nonverbal communication, it cannot stop it.

The Benefits of *SOAP Notes*

Indicator of Content Learning

With masks now off, I continued *SOAP Notes* when teaching rhetorical devices. During discussion of rhetorical terms, I observed students' looping gaze: attending to me as I spoke or wrote on the board → typing content onto their rhetoric term handout → looking at the board or me for the next example when they were ready. Their board or returned eye contact to me disclosed that they were ready to discuss the next term—a much more expedient and less intrusive process than constantly asking, "Are you ready to discuss the next term?"

As the rhetoric lesson continued, an interesting nonverbal dynamic occurred that ended up revealing an indicator of content learning. I mispronounced the word "anaphora," which is the repetition of a word or phrase at the beginning of phrases, clauses, or sentences, such as in Lincoln's Gettysburg Address: "we can not dedicate—we can not consecrate—we can not hallow—this ground." Fortunately, I got corrected. Like my students, when I learn a new word or pronunciation, I get to add it to the vocabulary board in the back of the room. Since this vocabulary learning process is a contest, students adding a word to their class period's list is marked by honor, joy, and enthusiasm. When I learn a new word or pronunciation, I am typically excited as well. However, this time, I honestly felt a bit ashamed that I wasn't more prepared for the lesson. I expected to turn around from the vocabulary wall and see intimations of a lack of respect for my knowledge or preparation, but I excitedly observed not one form of student body language indicative of such feelings but additionally, smiles and enthusiastic gestures. What a blessing to model the joy of learning voice free of judgment and fear!

Rather, they were smiling excitedly that I, too, had learned a new pronunciation. Calmed by their nonverbal responses, my loud, enthusiastic, "I say, class repeats!" echoing soon extinguished... echoing soon extinguished the old pronunciation as we increased the fun as we learned together. Our mutual enthusiasm then spurred intense thumbs up (ready), thumbs down (not ready) or flat hand (almost ready) responses when I asked if they were now ready to learn the definition of "anaphora." The intensity of their gestures proved to be an indicator of higher student interest and ultimate efficacy in learning the term "anaphora."

Overall, students' forward-leaning body position and smiling facial expressions after my mistake spurred my enthusiastic reaction that synergistically increased the class learning culture, thus leading to more successful learning as this rhetoric term proved to be the most used in students' later writings, both in essays and poetry. Consequently, *SOAP Notes* revealed that the more intense the student body movements and gesturing, the stronger the student–teacher culture and students' alacrity for and success in learning.

Indicator of Student–Teacher Relationship

To my amazement, the reflective and analytical practice inherent in *SOAP Notes* afforded further epiphanies beyond the symbiotic nonverbal communication relationship between students and teacher which catalyzes student learning. If positive student nonverbal communication forges teacher confidence and comfortability (even in a veteran teacher), then positive teacher nonverbal communication (especially toward students with low self-esteem or anxiety) must assuredly forge student confidence, risk-taking, and comfortability. Conversely, negative nonverbal communication likely hinders the student–teacher relationship, and thus student growth and learning. Therefore, teacher non-verbal reactions to students' mistakes have the power to accelerate or hinder student learning.

Indicator of Class Culture

These prior epiphanies made me wonder if *SOAP Notes* could confirm Frisby and Martin's (2010) positive correlation between teacher–student and student–student rapport and student success. Because an overwhelmingly safe, positive, and embracing environment maximizes learning, could *SOAP Notes* serve as a barometer of class culture and, thus, learning efficacy?

If students feel comfortable and safe to be themselves, then the higher the likelihood that their nonverbal communication—some of which is conscious and some of which may be subconscious—accurately depicts themselves as a learner and individual. Alternatively, when students do not feel safe and confident to be themselves among their peers and teacher, their nonverbal communication may be a protective façade that does not accurately portray who they are as people and learners. Therefore, the more genuinely students' nonverbal communication depicts themselves as a student, the more accurately informed the teacher is to make well-founded decisions that catalyze, and even catapult, learning.

Class Culture

Testing *SOAP Notes'* Accuracy in Detecting Class Culture

I noticed that the higher scoring (as determined by end-of-unit summative assessments) class period of my junior honors English course displayed more positive and more frequent actions of nonverbal communication. For example, when I change seats at the beginning of each unit, I tell my students to thank their side partner with a specific compliment, then give a high five, fist bump, or even a hug if they feel so moved. The higher-scoring of the two sections had 100 percent participation giving compliments and more vigorous fist bumps and high fives between each set of side partners, with two sets of side partners choosing to hug and another two sets with sad facial expressions as they leaned into each other and gently touched heads or shoulders for several seconds as they said goodbye. In contrast, my *SOAP Notes* indicated that the length of time of the lower-scoring section was shorter as their compliments and physical interactions were more brief.

SOAP Notes revealed that further indicators of strong class culture include sustained and direct eye contact and light touches on the forearm or shoulder, as well as glances with other students followed by smiles to the teacher and among students. Finally, as side partners sat in groups of four, I noticed that groups with strong, supportive (emotionally and academically) relationships more frequently turned or leaned toward each other to smile, fist bump, or high five as they discussed literature and strove for consensus while respecting the diversity of opinions. A class culture in which students feel safe enough to risk and be vulnerable with their ideas and feelings forges this beneficial academic bond.

Student Seating Dynamic as Indicator of Class Culture and Catalyst for Academic Growth

I assign seats for virtually every unit based on a variety of indicators: students' prior performance on the power standards prioritized in the upcoming unit, plus what I have learned about each student because of our relationship (i.e., learning preferences, social-emotional strengths and weaknesses, demeanor, leadership skills, current social-emotional state, personal interests, and life experiences). I consult my prior seating charts to ensure that no partners have been paired before because I think it's important for students to learn how to work well with all others. Needless to say, figuring out the seating chart for each unit takes me considerable time, especially as the school year wears on and I have more prior seating charts to consult. Because of this time factor, I've often considered abandoning this practice. Could hours of my time be used more wisely to increase student growth?

Wondering, I focused my reflective practice on the nonverbal behavior between partners, hoping *SOAP Notes* would verify that strong partner rapport throughout the class would correspond with higher summative assessment scores. Ultimately, would *SOAP Notes* confirm that I should not abandon my frequent change of assigned seating practices because it increases student learning? But how much of learning is really affected by seating? Behan (2019) states, "the seating chart is an underrated tool that can help turn a good learning environment into a great one" (para. 15).

So, I observed the nonverbal communication between partners after switching their seats for the new unit. The first partner work involved sharing their annual goals (academic, English, and personal) and goal progress. The majority of the students in the lower-performing class period paused 2–8 seconds before discussing. As well, they shared by turning only their heads to speak to their new partner. Whereas, all but one set of partners in the higher-scoring section shared within two seconds, and all turned not only their head but also their shoulders and for some, even their entire body toward their new partner. Furthermore, they spent longer time reading, discussing, and analyzing the progress on their goals. Therefore, a stronger relationship amongst students can be determined from just nonverbal partner communication. The rapid speed with which they raise their hands, move to work with others, engage in an activity, or respond to my or their peers' thoughts, ideas, and questions highlighted the *lack* of alacrity in other students' movements. I would have never thought to look at the absence of movement as an indicator of subpar class culture.

My *SOAP Notes* reflection informed my teaching practice: I need to continue spending time on my seating charts and work harder in my other class period to forge the classroom bonds and sense of belonging that transports students to higher levels of academic success. Thus, for the currently lower-scoring section of students, I planned a five-minute fun bonding activity every week. I look forward to observing nonverbal cues of their increased bond and trust in their partner, fellow students, and me, for these are the precursors of quality discussion and learning.

Symbiotic Nonverbal Communication Maximizes Learning

The *SOAP Notes* Experiment Reversed

After my *SOAP Notes* practice ended, I stood enthralled as I realized how much student nonverbal communication impacted teacher decisions that increased learning. Such success made me ponder: How does *my* nonverbal communication impact the learning process for students? Intrigued, I asked my students—with no benefit of receiving any points for the course, mind you—if they would mind filling out *SOAP Notes* about *my* nonverbal communication and how it informs them. Thankfully, 31 out of 48 students followed through, and I must admit, they were more observant than I was. Their feedback is quite compelling in corroborating that teacher nonverbal communication also informs the learning process, affecting student success in advantageous or deleterious ways.

As patterns emerged from my students' *SOAP Notes*, I realized that certain types of nonverbal communication seemed linked to particular student emotional or learning needs in their educational experience. To highlight these patterns, so the charts can be utilized in an instructive manner for teachers, I categorized certain types of teacher nonverbal communication that can effectively address specific student learning needs.

Positive Student Socioemotional Health as a Precursor for Learning

One pattern that emerged related to student socioemotional health. Maslow (1943) informs us that self-actualization is predicated on safety and belonging needs being met. Therefore, students' sense of safety and belonging in the classroom are precursors to learning and growing into their best student and self. Student *SOAP Notes* revealed that it's not just their classmates' nonverbal communication (i.e., head nods for approval, smiles) that engender safety and a sense of belonging but also their teachers' nonverbal communication. For example, one student confided that

> when I'm taking a risk and answering a question in class, sometimes I look at you for guidance just to see if I'm correct, and you always give an encouraging head nod which I find super useful especially if I'm unsure.

Further student *SOAP Notes* revealed a multitude of teacher nonverbal behaviors that can increase their social-emotional needs in the classroom (see Table 11.1).

TABLE 11.1 *SOAP Notes*

Type of Nonverbal Behavior	Student-Observed Teacher Nonverbal Communication	Student SOAP Reflections and Perceptions
Student Need: Safety		
Facial Expression	Smile	◆ "Safe learning environment" ◆ "Creates a sense of familiarity" ◆ "Feel able to come ask any questions or to talk in class" ◆ "Makes me feel good and comfortable" ◆ "I feel a lot more welcomed to share my thoughts every day knowing there will not be airs of annoyance at any answers."
Speed and Intensity of Movement	Speed of delivery: slower, calmer nonverbal gestures and softened eye contact match slower, calmer verbal delivery Intense, well-intentioned movement	"When classmates, the teacher, or I discuss serious issues in our lives, she always sounds super earnest and takes her time to say what she has to say when she is being sincere and to listen calmly and sustain long, easy eye contact. This makes us feel safe to share." "Very expressive movements and emotions seem very genuine and real. Feels like I trust that her nonverbal communication aligns with her true thoughts and feelings, which creates trust in the classroom."
Gestures	Head nodding	◆ "When she is invested in or agrees with what someone is saying" ◆ "When students share their worries" ◆ "Gives a sense of reassurance" ◆ "This little gesture can do a lot to calm down a student who may be worried if what they are saying makes sense"
Student Need: Personal Sense of Belonging		
Body Position	Body lean toward student	"Makes me feel heard"
Eye Contact	Strong eye contact "Widened and attentive eyes"	"Makes me feel heard" "Shows you are listening intently to me, to us"

As students see us each day, we can choose to ease their stress and anxiety from whatever issues they've been dealing with during the school day or at home. *SOAP Notes* reveal that our smiles are irreplaceable. Empathic and effective teachers care greatly about their students, so why not let them know we care with a simple smile that tells them so much: you are safe; you are cared for? Even if mask-wearing or student absences mitigate this opportunity, we can respectively tell students that we are glad they are in class or send an email letting them know they were missed. Proximal, directly connected forms of teacher nonverbal communication acknowledge beyond student safety, affirming the power and worth of their presence and participation.

Embedding Nonverbal Communication into the Classroom

SOAP Notes on student or teacher nonverbal communication conclusively increase a multitude of learning indicators as well as learning itself, embedding nonverbal communication into the classroom routine provides teachers with a daily tool to optimize student growth and learning. More specifically, *SOAP Notes* reveal that some forms of nonverbal communication *immediately* reveal both students' academic learning status and social-emotional state; therefore, in order to inform our instruction more adeptly, nonverbal communication must be embedded into the learning process. Here are some informal assessment strategies that embed nonverbal communication daily.

Adapted Thumbs Up, Thumbs Down
As I model the hand gesture (e.g., thumbs up, flat hand, thumbs down), I describe what each gesture means in regard to the level of understanding for the standard, skills, or concepts being taught, so their responses inform my instruction on the spot. This allows for immediate teacher instructional changes such as providing further explanations or examples, or proceeding with the lesson based on student self-perceived mastery.

Continuum of Learning

This is a physical manifestation of an exit slip wherein students stand on a continuum of learning "line" described by the teacher. This snapshot informs tomorrow's differentiated instruction. This also works as a four corners activity, but I find that students are loath to stand in a corner by themselves and much more willing to stand next to a classmate on a line, which then provides more accurate informal self-assessment.

Elbow Exit Partners

At the end of class, students are told to find an elbow partner and share one to three things they learned that day. As I observe all students, the amount of movement (animation or lack thereof) in body language, length of engagement, shoulder turn facing their partner, eye contact, and head position (confident head up or unconfident lowered head) inform me of who might need more instruction or clarification. I can immediately move toward these students and address their learning needs and questions so they leave class with clarification versus confusion.

Conclusion

SOAP Notes indicate that every student and teacher action, eyebrow raise, body position, and gesture can facilitate or hinder not only learning but also the student–teacher relationship and class culture that are the gateways to learning. Because some teachers' nonverbal behaviors are intentional, whereas others may be subconscious, it is unlikely that we, as teachers, can fathom the myriad of our nonverbal communications that impact students. However, *SOAP Notes* provide an opportunity for teachers to analyze student nonverbal communication to inform teaching practices and can even be completed by students so teachers can plan and implement specific forms of nonverbal communication to maximize learning.

In addition, the reflection process that *SOAP Notes* affords is equally effective, thus reinforcing the synergistic, symbiotic relationship that summits academic performance. Because *SOAP Notes* attest that learning is magnified when nonverbal communication is a two-way teacher–student process, teachers must model the nonverbal communication we wish to see so students and teacher can trust each other's nonverbal behaviors. This trust is the foundation of the learning relationship. Without relational learning, academic success will flounder. With it, learning will soar.

Ending Thoughts

SOAP Notes on nonverbal forms of communication indicate so much more than I thought they would: students' willingness to participate, their level of understanding, their current demeanor and attitude, and their willingness to engage in the learning process as individuals and as a collective entity. Sometimes students' specific nonverbal communication was exactly what I expected, but sometimes it was not. Sometimes it confounded and challenged me, which created the most growth for me because it called on me to discover, then plan and act on what I needed to know as an educator. As educators—professionals dedicated to the craft of teaching—I encourage you to use *SOAP Notes* to observe a specific aspect of your instructional dynamic. Reflect on it. The extra time utilizing that information to improve instruction will be well worth it.

TAKE-AWAYS

SOAP Notes **reflective practice helped:**

- ◆ Confirm nonverbal student responses
- ◆ Enhance class culture
- ◆ Strengthen student–teacher and student–student learning

References

Behan, K. (2019). Create a culture, not a classroom: Why seating charts matter for student success. *Edsurge Teaching & Learning*. https://www.edsurge.com/news/2019-08-17-create-a-culture-not-a-classroom-why-seating-charts-matter-for-student-success

Frisby, B. N., & Martin, M. M. (2010). Instructor–student and student–student rapport in the classroom. *Communication Education*, *59*(2), 146–164.

Maslow, A. H. (1943). A theory of human motivation. *Psychological Review*, 50(4), 370–396.

Sparks, S. D. (2019, March 13). Why teacher–student relationships matter. *Education Week*. https://www.edweek.org/teaching-learning/why-teacher-student-relationships-matter/2019/03

12

Third Grade Challenges

State Testing, Text Connections, and Reflective Practice

Sarah Campbell

GETTING TO KNOW THE AUTHOR

♦ Elementary teacher
♦ 5th year of teaching
♦ Suburban school

I completed my *SOAP Notes* during my English Language Arts (ELA) block. I chose to record my notes on the reading passage portion because reading is such a huge focus in third grade. Third grade is known as a transitional year for students regarding their reading; students are no longer "learning to read," they are "reading to learn." When writing my *SOAP Notes*, the passages I chose to read with my students were intentionally selected, keeping state reading assessment preparation in mind (Ohio Department of Education, 2022).

The first five days of *SOAP Notes* reflect on a paired passage text set about tornadoes. On the first and second days, students

DOI: 10.4324/9781003493464-20

read a nonfiction passage about tornadoes, then answered comprehension questions. On the third and fourth days, students read a realistic fiction passage about a tornado and answered comprehension questions. On the fifth day, we reread the two passages and answered questions that related to both passages. The paired passages came in a set of paired passages that have been very engaging and high interest for our students throughout the school year. Although these passages and questions take a long time to complete with students, they have been an invaluable resource for my third-grade team as we prepare for state testing.

State testing material often includes paired passages students read and comprehension questions students respond to. After completing the tornado paired passages, we completed paired passages about pumpkins that my students really enjoyed. While reading passages and answering questions with my class, I always tried to extend students' learning beyond simple, explicit questions and connect our learning to other subjects, previous conversations, and experiences my students have had.

While reflecting on my *SOAP Notes*, I noticed when reading the tornado paired passages, I was impressed with students' abilities to make text connections while reading early on in the week. This led me to think about what deeper level thinking questions I could ask. Looking at my *SOAP Notes*, I noticed that as the week went on, I encouraged students to think about even more challenging questions such as, "What is a major problem in the story versus a minor problem?" I have noticed that when students are able to think deeply about what they are reading and make interdisciplinary and personal connections, they seem to retain information more effectively and typically do a better job when answering questions.

Days 6 through 12 of my *SOAP Notes* focused on nonfiction passages about Thanksgiving. My third grade team and I focus our comprehension passages on holidays and important dates throughout the year, and my *SOAP Notes* coincided with Thanksgiving week. Each year, the Thanksgiving text set is one of the first big opportunities students have for learning and comprehending specific academic vocabulary. We spend a lot of time

learning and practicing how to understand challenging vocabulary words in third grade by using a variety of strategies. We
often focus on using context clues, root words, and affixes to
understand the meaning of unknown words.

Again while reflecting on my *SOAP Notes*, I was proud of
my students' abilities to make text connections to passages we
have previously read. The more we read about Thanksgiving,
the more connections students made. Some of the passages
include information about the *Mayflower*, Mayflower Compact,
Squanto, and the First Thanksgiving. In my opinion, one of the
most exciting text connections students made is explained on
page nine of my *SOAP Notes* (see Table 12.1). The day before,

TABLE 12.1 *SOAP Notes*

S	**Subjective**: *students' willingness to participate, demeanor, body language, attitude. Teacher's perceptions and reflections*
	◆ Students really enjoy that these passages build off of each other, and we can make text connections between passages and what they have learned in years past. ◆ Students were excited to infer what the Mayflower Compact was before reading the passage based off of what we know about the word "compact" and what the picture is showing. ◆ While reading, we pulled some important vocabulary words from the passage, like *Mayflower* and Pilgrims. ◆ We made some text connections while reading since we are learning about government in social studies, and the passage talked about how the Mayflower Compact was the rules the Pilgrims decided to follow. ◆ We had a great discussion about how 41 men signed the Mayflower Compact, but yesterday we learned 101 Pilgrims came over from England on the *Mayflower*.
O	**Observation** of student learning: anecdotal notes
	◆ Students were able to define the words *"Mayflower"* and "Pilgrims" based on what we read about previously. ◆ Students were able to make the connection between the Mayflower Compact and the Constitution after I guided their thinking with questioning strategies. ◆ Students were able to infer why only 41 Pilgrims signed the Mayflower Compact when 101 Pilgrims traveled over on the Mayflower—they guessed women and children didn't vote or some people didn't agree with the Mayflower Compact.

(Continued)

TABLE 12.1 (Continued)

_A_	**Assessing** student learning: progress monitoring, running records, oral or written comprehension
	◆ These questions were only true and false, so we didn't have to write in complete sentences. ◆ We discussed what true and false means and found textual evidence to support why each answer is true or false. ◆ I walked around while we activated prior knowledge, and while we were answering questions, which I think helped students stay on task.
_P_	**Planning** for next lesson: use bullet points
	◆ I was really happy with all of the text connections and vocabulary discussion I had with students today. I want to know how I can continue to get students thinking like this in future passages.

Challenges: What challenges did you encounter while working with your students?
◆ No major challenges today

Further Learning: What else do you need to know how to do?
◆ How can I get students activating prior knowledge and thinking about vocabulary in future passages?

Source: Weaver, J. C., Hartzog, M., Murnen, T., & Bertelsen, C. D. (2019). Bowling Green State University.

we read about how 101 Pilgrims came over on the Mayflower. We learned about the few Pilgrims who died during the travels, and the students subtracted these Pilgrims from the 101 Pilgrims on the Mayflower. The next day, we read about the Mayflower Compact and learned that 41 men signed the compact.

This sparked excellent discussion with my students. The students wanted to discuss why only men signed the Mayflower Compact and completed a subtraction equation to determine how many women and children were probably on the _Mayflower_. We were able to have an excellent discussion about why only men signed the compact and how women's right to vote has changed over the years. According to what was written in my _SOAP Notes_, I was proud of my students for making these observations, and

I was really impressed with the conversations we had after reading these passages. When my students and I have conversations like these, I feel confident that the information they are learning is sticking in their brain more concretely than when we simply read a passage and answer the questions.

Something else I began to query in *Further Learning* was: "How could I get students thinking even more deeply about what they have read? Could I have students come up with their own questions to ask their peers based on the Thanksgiving passages?" This could include offering opportunities for students to infer about their own learning from the passages based on what we have already learned. Once we read a few passages about Thanksgiving, students were able to see how the information from one passage connected to the next passage. I believe having these conversations with students also helps build their vocabulary.

After the first of the year, I was excited to make text connections to other topics we have talked about throughout the year. As I mentioned earlier, I think making text connections helps students fully understand and commit to memory what they are learning. This led me to think about how I could plan more intentionally for next year and connect what we are reading in ELA to what we are learning in other subjects and what students have learned in second grade.

Upon reflection, my *SOAP Notes* showed me that a huge focus when reading passages in my classroom is making text connections with students. Since my third grade team and I try to expose students to a wide variety of reading topics, making text connections is an invaluable way to help students truly embed their learning in their long-term memories. My hope is that through wide reading opportunities and by making text connections, students will have some sort of text connection or background knowledge they can use when reading passages on state assessments.

Additionally, I noticed a recurring theme toward the beginning of my *SOAP Notes* of students struggling to write answers in complete sentences. This has been a continuous struggle this school year. My student teacher and I have found that students are able to explain what a complete sentence is and are able to come up with excellent sentence starters and stems. Additionally, they can verbally answer a question in a complete sentence. When it comes down to students actually writing the complete sentence, many students do not. This has been a struggle all school year in my classroom as well as the other third grade classrooms. The other third grade teachers and I are trying to figure out how to solve this problem and have yet to come up with a solution that consistently works other than constantly reminding the students who do not write in complete sentences that they must write in complete sentences in third grade and beyond.

Through reflective practice using *SOAP Notes*, I feel that I have become more effective at being more intentional with the reading passages I am selecting, as well as how to best prepare students for the challenging state assessments. There is not an exact formula for how to best prepare students to be success-ful in third grade, but I feel strongly that reflecting on what my students and I do every day in our classroom is a great start. Additionally, I believe spending time intentionally reflecting on my practices allows me to continuously evaluate student learn-ing, struggles and successes, and what I can do to help students continue to progress as the year continues.

My suggestion for elementary educators is to not shy away from the challenges associated with third grade and to use reflec-tive practice to strengthen student comprehension through inten-tional decision-making. In my experience, it is very rewarding working with students in such a pivotal year and seeing students learn new concepts. Through writing *SOAP Notes*, I thought it was amazing to reflect on students' deeper thinking and their growth in learning while making text connections. Although the pressures of the third grade state assessments are always in the back of my mind, reflecting on my practices as an educator and constantly striving to be the most effective third grade teacher is my ultimate goal. Recording and analyzing *SOAP Notes* for 15 days definitely helped me continue to improve myself as an educator who engages in reflective practice.

TAKE-AWAYS

SOAP Notes **reflective practice helped:**

♦ Build confidence in instructional decision-making
♦ Focus on challenges to support deeper thinking of students
♦ Create intentionality in passage selection
♦ Focus on effective reading strategies to support student success on state assessments

---

References

Ohio Department of Education. (2022, January 14). *Third Grade Reading Guarantee*. https://education.ohio.gov/Topics/Learning-in-/Literacy/Third-Grade-Reading-Guarantee

13

The Power of Reflection

Grace Mutti

GETTING TO KNOW THE TEACHER

◆ 8th grade ELA teacher
◆ 1st year of teaching
◆ Suburban and urban middle school
◆ Range of reading levels: 2nd–11th grade

Being a first-year teacher is hard. This is where reflection and *SOAP Notes* come in. You have your student teaching experiences to reflect on but no experience establishing a positive classroom environment from scratch. A lot of times, the majority of the content is new. If you're lucky, maybe you see some similarities between your student teaching classes and your first official class of students. Maybe you can reuse some of your content from student teaching. But odds are, your new group of students will come in with completely different learning needs than the group you taught during student teaching, the content will be different in topic and scope, and this time it is up to you to sort through the curriculum maps, connect with other teachers, and choose the content and instructional strategies that will work in *your* classroom with *your* students.

DOI: 10.4324/9781003493464-21

My use of *SOAP Notes* reflection on student engagement and the effectiveness of my instructional strategies will be the foundation of my teaching career, and it is my hope that as the years go by, my ability to reflect and adapt will allow me to overcome all my new teacher fears and insecurities, help me establish confidence in my instructional choices and ultimately become a better teacher. By using the *SOAP Notes* framework, I am hopeful that I will come back stronger, more confident, and better prepared for the challenges of next year.

Implementation of *SOAP Notes*

This chapter will highlight my discoveries about students in an 8th Grade Language Arts classroom and provide insight into the ups and downs that many first-year teachers experience. I reflected using the *SOAP Notes* template for three classes during which students were wrapping up personal narratives and transitioning into our horror unit featuring three central texts: *The Monkey's Paw* by W. W. Jacobs, *The Tell-Tale Heart* by Edgar Allan Poe, and *The Legend of Sleepy Hollow* by Washington Irving. Prior to this unit, students completed a separate unit on short stories where they explored characterization, identified instances of character development, and examined the structure of a narrative. Characterization, character development, and narrative structure were also a focus of my horror unit; however, in this unit, I challenged students to dig deeper into these concepts. Instead of focusing on surface-level character traits and how the characters changed, I pushed students to think about the choices the authors made to develop the characters, plot, and ultimately theme. Throughout my 15 days of recorded *SOAP Notes*, I learned a lot about my students' strengths, weaknesses, and interests as well as my own instructional strengths and weaknesses. It was these discoveries about my students and myself that demonstrate the positive impact of reflection on instruction.

On day one of my notes, I had just given students their first STAR assessment of the year. This assessment was recommended to me by the other teachers and my principal to track student growth and identify student strengths and weaknesses. From this assessment, it became clear that my students' strengths and weaknesses widely varied, and their attitude toward the test might have affected their performance. Also, I learned very quickly that while the assessment was new to me, it was not new to my students.

The day of the STAR test, the students came in excited, but when I told them we were doing STAR tests, the energy in the room immediately shifted. The excited chatter turned into griping and groaning, and one student even told me it was, "The worst thing I could have [them] do" (*SOAP Notes* Day 1). Looking through the results, I noticed that my students' scores had an extremely wide range, but many were low and did not seem to reflect their academic abilities. It was fairly early in the year, so I couldn't be sure that their attitude toward the tests was a central factor in their score, but I did already get the sense that a different assessment might provide different (and possibly better) results.

Impact on Student Learning

The majority of my students disliked traditional tests; however, they were much more engaged with topics they were already familiar with, class discussions, and activities featuring technology. When I introduced the horror unit on day five, students were highly engaged with the topic and technology incorporated into the lesson. I made a note that several students who do not typically speak up in class chimed in when asked to share their experiences with horror novels and movies and while identifying characteristics of the horror genre in short video clips.

My students were much more engaged in these types of activities; however, the increased engagement often brought in new challenges with classroom management and talking out, discussed in my *SOAP Notes* on day 15. Students shared their fiction, nonfiction, and legend foldables or their retellings of *The Tell Tale Heart*. On day 15, I motivated students to complete their writing assignment by bringing in Halloween treats and giving them an opportunity to share their work with their peers. Like day 5, there was a significant increase in student engagement; however, my students struggled with focusing and/or listening for long periods of time, and this challenge was apparent in the Challenges section of my *SOAP Notes*.

Impact on Instruction

I learned a lot about my students' strengths, weaknesses, and interests through my *SOAP Notes*, but I learned a significant amount about myself and my instruction as well. The first realization I had about myself was that my instruction was affected far more by my collection of reflective observational notes through *SOAP Notes* rather than test results. For example, when I discovered that students disliked STAR tests, I engaged them more in this activity by setting goals and conferencing with them about their results on future STAR tests. My students didn't all respond in the same way, but several students from each class expressed interest in learning more about their scores, the trends in their data, and topics of focus before the next STAR test. For me, this was extremely rewarding because I had found a way to make students slightly more interested (or at least curious) about something they initially expressed complete disinterest in.

Based on my *SOAP Notes* reflections, I adjusted learning activities my students disliked to make the activities more student-centered and engaging. I tried to expand and build on my students' interests as well. For example, I made the decision to add *The Legend of Sleepy Hollow* into my horror unit specifically because my students seemed to enjoy horror. I also knew that they would enjoy watching and analyzing the film version given their engagement with the video activity on day five. By personalizing students' STAR test experiences and intentionally incorporating high-interest materials into my classroom, I have demonstrated a strong focus on the emotional responses of students to the content and my instruction because of using *SOAP Notes*.

Does this mean that I completely neglect the test scores? No. The grading process has provided me with valuable insights about student understanding and areas of growth that have shaped my instruction. While grades on assessments do provide me with valuable information about what students have truly learned, I must wait much longer and work much harder for that data than I do for my *SOAP Notes* reflections. Student responses to content and instruction are immediate.

I am fully aware that my instruction cannot be entirely driven by students' responses to content and instruction, but so far, my *SOAP Notes* have been very helpful in getting a general idea of what my students know, what they don't know, and what they would be interested in learning more about. I can use my reflections to inform my immediate day-to-day instruction.

SOAP Notes have helped me become aware of my ability to build strong relationships with my students and design engaging activities, but they have also made me aware of my weaknesses. Pacing has been a huge challenge for me because, as a first-year teacher, I frequently struggle with deciding when it is necessary to step back and reteach and when it is more beneficial to simply continue pushing forward. For example, when I was wrapping up the personal narratives during days two, three, and four, I had to make the decision to push students to finish their narratives despite their lack of progress. This was a difficult decision for me to make because I knew that some students would not finish, and I do not enjoy seeing my students fail; however, I knew that students needed to see the consequences of their choice to waste time. Otherwise, valuable instruction time would continue to be wasted.

On day 4, when I told students I would not be extending the deadline, it became clear to me that because I had extended deadlines on a few assignments in the past, they viewed these prior extensions as permission to slack off instead of seeing them as opportunities to improve the quality of their work. It is likely that my students had also begun to expect these extensions that would only lead to more pacing issues if I failed to address the issue. The full-class discussion that took place because of this decision was not fun, but there was a definitive shift in my students' focus and attention to their work during that class period because they knew that this time I was not going to back off. I know that in the future, I need to make sure I continue reinforcing my expectations for them to take advantage of class time by showing them what will happen if they don't.

At this point in my career, I am still building my frame of reference for where my eighth graders "should be." I don't want my expectations to be unattainable, but I also don't want them to be too low. Constantly questioning 8th grade expectations has contributed to my struggle with pacing. Despite this struggle, I hope that with more time and experience, I will be able to build my frame of reference and improve in this area. The majority of the *Challenges* and *Further Learning* sections of my *SOAP Notes* are filled with comments and questions regarding student attitudes, challenging behaviors, and a lack of motivation and/or self-confidence. Similar to pacing, it is my hope that time and experience will equip me with the necessary strategies and scripts to deal with these challenges as well.

Overall, *SOAP Notes* reflection has significantly shaped the content and instructional strategies I incorporated across a unit, and it will definitely serve me well next year as I adapt to an entirely new group of students. This year, I have learned that my students' reading abilities range from 2nd to 11th grade, that they have a unique blend of learning styles that shifts from one student to the next, and that there is a wide range of challenges students face at home and in the classroom. As for myself, I have learned that I am good (for the most part) at establishing connections with my students and finding new ways to motivate them and engage them with the content.

I still have a long way to go when it comes to developing behavioral and academic expectations at the eighth grade level and using assessment results to guide my instruction, but with time and more *SOAP Notes* reflection, I hope to work through these challenges. I want to be an effective and confident teacher who stands by each decision I make; I want to be a better teacher who knows with her entire being that she belongs in this profession. With time, experience, and reflection, I hope to be all these things.

TAKE-AWAYS

SOAP Notes **reflective practice positively impacted:**

◆ Teacher's confidence in her instructional choices
◆ Knowledge of students' strengths, weaknesses, emotional learning, and interests
◆ Teacher's ability to establish rapport and support student learning
◆ Student learning during small group work
◆ Student goal-setting and participation

Challenges and Further Learning sections encouraged:

◆ Questioning around teaching practices, student attitudes, motivation, and/or self-confidence

Student Needs Revealed through *SOAP Notes*

14

The (Wo)man, the Myths, and the Legend(ary) Lessons

Elizabeth Kikel

GETTING TO KNOW THE AUTHOR

♦ Middle school English
♦ 3rd year of teaching
♦ Urban school district

As I sit at my cluttered desk, in my cluttered classroom, with my cluttered mind, I ask myself, "How did I get here?" As a teacher who started her teaching career when the pandemic hit, I have learned an insurmountable amount about myself, my teaching practices, and how to lead my classroom with love, patience, and forgiveness even in the worst of times. For this reason, I chose my 7th grade girls reading and English class to reflect upon using *SOAP Notes*.

During my two weeks of reflective teaching, I focused on RACE writing, which is a practice commonly used at Jones Leadership to make sure students are answering questions completely and accurately. Naturally, it's an acronym because teachers love acronyms. Students focused on Restating the question,

DOI: 10.4324/9781003493464-23

Answering the question, Citing the evidence, and Explaining the evidence. On the first day of my *SOAP Notes*, students focused on note taking using "doodle notes," a more creative form of note-taking that involves a lot of coloring.

I have found in the past that if you give the students more than one sentence to write during traditional note taking, they will complain until the bell rings. But if you give them coloring sheets with a significant amount more of writing, they will happily doodle their sweet little hearts out. Starting with something engaging sets the tone for the rest of the unit. While we started slow and steady with doodle notes, we worked our way into applying our knowledge to actual questions that needed to be answered. The largest factors that I honed in on during my *SOAP Notes* were the students' confidence levels, formative assessments, behavior management, and interactive activities that allowed the students to get more involved.

I took note of my students' confidence levels or lack thereof because it was an important factor in their growing success during the lessons. On the very first day, I took note of their lack of confidence with higher level comprehension questions. I wanted to monitor this as we progressed throughout the next several weeks (see Figure 14.1).

By day 3, I noted that the students were not necessarily confident in their answers but felt comfortable enough to share and even make mistakes (see Figure 14.2).

I chalk this up to positive reinforcement and relationships in my classroom. Students were willing to ask questions when they didn't understand the material. Without establishing a positive rapport within the classroom, these little moments would not be possible, and this would hinder students ability to learn in class. By day 6, I observed that students were feeling more confident within their own abilities because they were quick to answer questions like, "What is the question word?" "How do you restate the question?" and "How do we answer the question?" This showed they were gaining confidence in their skills. Something incredibly important that I noted was that we did not get as far as I had planned, but I would rather go slow and steady versus moving forward and not having students understand.

S	Subjective: students' willingness to participate, demeanor, body language, attitude. Teacher's perceptions and reflections

- Doodle notes: we have done them before? the kids enjoy them
  - took from Tpt
  - positive attitudes? enjoy the calming of coloring
- I LOVE doodle notes bc it gives students something to do once they are done writing
  - Great for classroom management

Q	Observation of student learning: anecdotal notes

- The students completed the doodle notes w/ ease. One student told me these calm her down while also being able to learn.

A	Assessing student learning: Progress monitoring, running records, oral or written comprehension

- Students volunteered to answer questions including:
  - how do we restate the question?
  - what is the question word?
  - how can we prove this?
  - They have less confidence in their higher level comprehension questions, but we are working on building that confidence.

P	Planning for next lesson: use bullet points

- Apply RACE writing strategy to story (All Summer in a day)
- Break it down: Day 1 (R 3A), Day 2 (C ʒ E)

	Challenges: What challenges did you encounter while working with your students?

- Students still struggle w/ the phones being a distraction
  - Working on keeping them engaged.
- Still working on note taking: They struggle to understand spatial things regarding notes

	Further Learning: What else do you need to know how to do?

FIGURE 14.1 *SOAP Notes*: Day 1

As I look back on this, this moment was imperative during the next few weeks of my planning because it would allow students the opportunity to gain confidence in their own abilities. Building the students' confidence as we continued on in future lessons not only helped students feel comfortable asking questions when needed but also students' confidence as we continued on in future lessons; it helped students feel comfortable not only asking questions gaining the ability to think critically and independently. I found it crucial to go at the students' pace as we ventured through these lessons to help the students succeed. Oftentimes, we, as educators, feel we must stick to a timeline because of expectations that are set on us. However, the most beneficial thing I could have done for my students during this time was *not* to push through in order to stick to a schedule, but

S	Subjective: students' willingness to participate, demeanor, body language, attitude. Teacher's perceptions and reflections
	• Students were nervous today because they knew they were sharing their 2 answers from yesterday w/ the class
	- this is strange to me considering they understood the work yesterday ? Volunteered yesterday
	- Then more resistant when answering // seem to doubt their abilities
	- Got more comfortable as they went on.
	• Students then had to review C 3 6 But did NOT apply it to the story yet.

O	Observation of student learning: anecdotal notes
	• While students were not confident, many correct answers were given.
	- good questions were also asked if they didn't understand.
	• Students did a great job volunteering when reviewing C3E
	• the biggest struggle was figuring out how to highlight on a Chromebook

A	Assessing student learning: Progress monitoring, running records, oral or written comprehension
	• Students came up to board to answer their 2 questions:
	- were asked to cross off the question word
	- were asked to restate the question
	- were asked to answer the question
	• 2 students seemed to fall back w/ participation; later revealed they struggled to understand R & A

P	Planning for next lesson: use bullet points
	• Review C 3 E (cite 3 explain)
	- apply to story (go back to previous worksheet 3 build on previous lessons)

Challenges: What challenges did you encounter while working with your students?
• It was difficult to keep students engaged while other students were up at the board.
- would begin to talk to one another
- how do you speed up the work to keep engaged or is their something to keep them engaged?

Further Learning: What else do you need to know how to do?

FIGURE 14.2 *SOAP Notes:* Day 3

to slow down and allow the students time to process information at their own pace. By the end of my *SOAP Notes*, I noted that students were volunteering their *own* answers without hesitation and without needing prompted. Evidently, slow and steady does win the race and gives students the confidence in themselves to help them flourish.

Formative assessments are an excellent tool when trying to reflect on lessons because it gives the chance for growth by meeting students at their individual needs. I started formative assessments early by giving the students the opportunity to give me a thumbs up, down, or sideways with their eyes closed to communicate how they felt on day 2 of RACE writing practice. I took note on *SOAP Notes* that over half felt confident in RACE writing, while the others wanted more time to grasp the concepts.

I continued to use this form of assessment because it was quick, easy, and allowed the students to be honest about their progress without feeling the need to lie about their progress in front of their peers. I continued the use of formative assessments in the form of "quick checks" that allowed me to check their work before allowing them to move on to the homework. This enabled me to give feedback on their work to reduce mistakes that may have been made on future work. Formative assessments were crucial during my *SOAP Notes* and provided me an opportunity to reflect on where I needed to reteach and modify my lessons.

Behavior management has always been something I have struggled with within the classroom. I wish I could say that by my third year, I have my act together, but many days feel like a losing battle—a very weird, confusing, "why are you barking as you come into my classroom?" battle. However, by reflecting on the issues that were happening, I was able to hone in on certain behaviors and create strategies that would help keep students stay engaged and less distracted by themselves and other outside factors. I have found that in their universe, the world certainly revolves around students, or at least, that's what they think. This can be critical to keep in mind as we reflect and create lessons.

Two major issues I tried to address were (1) keeping students invested even when it wasn't their turn to speak and (2) *cell phones* (and the classroom expectations surrounding them). I could write a whole novel about cell phones in the classroom. Truthfully, I could probably re-create many of the dances that are on TikTok solely because of the amount of times I have had to watch my students "drop it like it is hot." Yes, I do tell them to stop, and yes, they do find me lame for using that phrase. One way to combat both of these issues is by giving the students interactive lessons including presentations, board work, and games. I noted several times throughout the process that students would turn to talk, get out their cell phones, or create distractions by simply moving around the room freely.

When I took note of these in my *SOAP Notes*, I was able to reflect back and decide how I wanted to address these issues in the future. Many times, these issues arrived during the days where students were sitting and learning or not being specifically involved in the learning process itself. On these days, I determined that the following day, a lesson itself would have to regroup the students. Two specific examples included allowing the students to play review games. The first review game was *Jeopardy*, which has been a recurring game in the classroom because the students *love* the competitive nature of it. The second review game was for vocabulary that allowed the students to break away from the RACE writing. These were some of the most enjoyable days because they just had fun. Testing and standards have become so prominent in the field of education that sometimes we forget to just have fun.

By giving the students the chance to enjoy themselves, scream a little, and kick a little butt, it allowed them to refocus the next few days as they reeled from the fun of the previous days. During the vocabulary review day, it broke away from the monotonous activities that gave students a "brain break," which I highly recommend in the classroom. By taking note of this on *SOAP Notes*, I have actively chosen to use review games and other forms of brain breaks to allow students the chance to just be kids in a safe and controlled environment.

Finally, interactive activities were imperative during the learning process, even if they weren't always successful. Throughout my *SOAP Notes* reflections, I tried several interactive activities including posters, presentations, and small group work. While I may not have been able to adjust my teaching for this unit by reflecting back on these lessons, I can adjust for future lessons. One of the biggest areas that I noticed needed improvement were the students' presentation skills. Often, we rely on other teachers to teach students basic skills like presenting, spelling, and so forth that sometimes I forget that I *am* the teacher who is supposed to teach them those various skills. Reflecting back on their presentations over the RACE writing strategy, I took note that many students struggled in similar areas including eye contact, volume, and confidence.

I made the assumption that students had learned these presentation skills in previous years; however, I was surely mistaken as we began our presentations. I took note that one of the presenters came up unprepared and wasted a lot of class time that eventually led me to taking over, so that students could obtain accurate information. In the future, I want to prepare students by giving them the skills they need to present information verbally to the class. This information is a vital skill for the classroom and also everyday life. We, as teachers, have the important responsibility to teach students how to function effectively in the real world. This includes being able to confidently communicate and speak on their own behalf. If they are not able to do this, they need to *at least* be able to fake it until they make it. By preparing the students more in the classroom, I am better able to equip them with the tools they need in order to be successful outside of the classroom.

I wish I could say that I felt confident in all of my lessons or that I know who I am as a teacher, but the fact of the matter is that every day I am learning and figuring it out. In a time when many teachers are quitting or questioning why they still teach, I am simply happy to come in every day and have the opportunity to interact with students who give me a sense of purpose. Not every lesson has been perfect. In fact, many of my lessons reflected upon in my *SOAP Notes* show what I could have done better. Something important I have learned about being a teacher is that you have to always want to be a lifelong learner. Do I know a whole lot? Maybe. Do I know at least a little bit? Absolutely. Is there room for improvement? *Always.* Over the course of my 26 years of learning, I have been inspired by many teachers, but the person who has influenced me most is my own mother, the original Ms. Kikel. She has always instilled in my mind that the moment you believe you are done learning is the day that you should leave education.

These *SOAP Notes* have reminded me that in order to grow as an educator, I have to lead with love and have the willingness to always do and be better for my students. Reflective teaching has shown me how to adjust my teaching style to meet the needs of my students, which ultimately will be different from the needs of other educators' students. But by completing the *SOAP Notes* reflection process, teachers, including myself, are able to hone in on how they can help their students succeed.

Being an English teacher isn't about knowing where to put punctuation, how to spell every word imaginable (thank goodness for spell check), or reading every Shakespeare play ever written. In fact, I still struggle with commas, have to google spellings, and passed my Shakespeare class with a C+. Those aspects are important, but being a teacher is about having the ability to reflect upon our own instruction and continue to want to inspire others around us even if we are not experts on every topic. I take pride in my ability to love, forgive, empathize, and care for others, including my students, even if I had to rely on the red squiggle line to determine if I used *there*, *their*, or *they're* throughout the entirety of this manuscript. I hope to continue using *SOAP Notes* reflective practice in my lesson planning to help my students find their passions, find success, and find a love for learning.

TAKE-AWAYS

SOAP Notes **reflective practice helped:**

- ♦ Build student confidence and success
- ♦ Students think critically
- ♦ Strengthen behavior management strategies
- ♦ Student engagement and motivation through interactive activities
- ♦ Build and strengthen writing strategies

15

Reflective Practice

Insights and Impact

Julianna Cajka

GETTING TO KNOW THE AUTHOR

- ♦ English/history teacher middle school
- ♦ 3rd year of teaching
- ♦ Christian school

Introduction

If there was one simple practice that could make you a better teacher, wouldn't you do it? If there was one small, systematic habit that was guaranteed to not only make you more effective at your job, but a wiser, more thoughtful person as well, you might think it was too good to be true, but how could you resist giving it a try anyway? In the following pages, I will outline some of my experiences with a practice that I have found to be both enlightening and impactful: daily reflective writing using the *SOAP Notes* framework.

DOI: 10.4324/9781003493464-24

Context

When I completed this project, I was a third-year teacher at a small Christian school in the suburbs. Like many schools, the students there represented a broad spectrum of backgrounds, life experiences, and academic abilities. My students were 7th graders, and although our language arts classes combine literature, writing, and mechanics, the lessons I focused for *SOAP Notes* were 15 consecutive days of grammar instruction. We were finished with subjects, verbs, and nouns and moving into less familiar territory: sentence complements, modifiers, and phrases. During this unit, many students were pushed beyond what was easy for them. Their reactions to this increasingly difficult content (and my attempts to support them in their various wrestling with the complexity that is the English language) provide the context for my reflections.

Insight 1: Student Engagement

As I completed my reflections each day, there were several areas that I thought about most frequently. One of these areas was student engagement. Davis (2012) argues that student engagement involves several dimensions: behavioral, cognitive, and relational. For a student to be truly engaged, he or she must not only follow instructions and complete assigned tasks (aspects of behavioral engagement) but actively think, process, and make connections (pp. 23–24). Securing student engagement is an obvious goal, but what specific changes can I make to achieve it? *SOAP Notes* reflective writing turned out to be a powerful tool in finding answers to this question.

As I started recording observations related to student engagement using the *SOAP Notes* template, I noticed a few patterns that would later become opportunities for growth. First, I realized that when I asked a question that was directed to the entire class, there were a few students who were always engaged. These students were willing to raise their hand to answer nearly any question I asked. I knew I had the engagement of at least these three or four students, but I started thinking about the students who did not raise their hand. Were they also engaged in these question-and-answer parts of the lesson? I also noticed that during times when I was just talking—not asking questions or directly involving the students besides expecting them to listen—engagement sagged. Oddly enough, when I was delivering (what I thought were) fascinating mini-lectures on such compelling topics as the distinction between definite and indefinite articles, the students were not as cognitively or behaviorally engaged as I might have hoped.

As a direct result of my *SOAP Notes* reflections (and a new-found and humbling realization that everything I say may not be as interesting as I think it is), I made two resolutions that shaped later lessons and continued to shape my teaching practice. First, I wanted to eliminate as much as I could the times when I expected students to just passively listen as I explained something. How could we explore the content in different, more active ways? Second, I wanted to use strategies that would involve not just a few students, but everyone in the class, or at least as many individual students as possible. How could I incorporate whole-class responses or assign jobs and tasks throughout the lesson to keep everyone involved?

For the first time, I started regularly borrowing a set of dry erase boards and markers from a neighboring teacher. I also incorporated interactive reading strategies, called students to write on the board, asked them to evaluate each other's work to give even more students a chance to be involved, and experimented with several other strategies that would give students opportunities to move, speak, and think, not just listen to me and two or three of their classmates. When I was honest with myself about what works and doesn't work to secure student engagement, I felt confident exchanging some of my default strategies for more creative new ones.

Insight 2: Understanding Student Thought Processes

A second area of interest for me as I completed my *SOAP Notes* reflections built on the first. As students became more actively engaged and shared more often what they were thinking, what happened when their answers were not correct? I began to realize that knowing any given answer required a fairly complicated combination of knowledge and skills, creating the possibility that a student might give an incorrect answer while still partially understanding the topic. For example, see the following sentence: *After school, I will brush my dog's fur*.

I might have half the class correctly identify the word *fur* as the direct object of this sentence. For the students who didn't get it correct, there could be multiple reasons why. Maybe they misidentified the verb (do they need more practice in what a verb is, the role it plays in the sentence, or where it is commonly found?). Did the confusion have something to do with the fact that the verb was future tense and had a helping verb in addition to the main verb? Maybe they identified the verb correctly, but they don't understand the difference between action and linking verbs, and how the type of verb relates to what type of complement is present. Or maybe they know all of this but just forgot what a direct object was. Doing *SOAP Notes* reflections gave me time to slow down and analyze the *why* behind student mistakes.

When I was younger, my mom used to have an annual fight with the lights on our Christmas tree. If even one bulb was burned out, the entire string would not light. She had to figure out which was the one bulb that was not working so the rest of the string would light up. Identifying students' misconceptions reminds me of my mom's Christmas lights. There may only be one bulb burned out, one small gap in knowledge, but it causes the whole answer to be incorrect. Once when I was working with an individual student, I noticed that he still seemed confused after my explanations. It was only later, when I completed my *SOAP Notes* reflection for the day, that I realized what the problem had been.

I had been inadvertently using a specialized, domain-specific word that I had not explicitly taught yet. We didn't have a shared vocabulary about the topic, and that was the one bulb that was causing the whole string to go dark. It was amazing to see the (figurative) lights come on as we figured out together how to identify the bulb that needed to be replaced. Pinpointing the specific reasons behind why students were missing answers via

SOAP Notes helped me to target their misconceptions, tailoring instruction each day so it was more closely aligned with what they actually needed to practice.

Insight 3: Correcting My Own Mistakes and Moving Forward

Making the occasional mistake is part of the learning process, and this is true for teachers as well as students. As a third year teacher, there are many mistakes I still make every day as I continue to gain experience. These mistakes range in size and intensity, and sometimes I don't even realize right away that something I did was ineffective. Writing *SOAP Notes* reflection on a daily basis can help teachers notice and correct these mistakes. My mistakes often involved informal assessment data that didn't provide the best picture of students' abilities.

One specific example of this occurred during a lesson on adjectives. The students had completed a workbook exercise where they were asked to underline the adjectives in practice sentences. They later checked their answers to see if they were right, but I didn't collect the assignment. I knew I needed some information on how they were doing, so before they checked their answers I asked, "How many adjectives did you find in sentence one?" They held up three, four, five, one, seven fingers . . . the correct answer was five. I was vaguely aware that something was wrong with this assessment, but it wasn't until later that evening when I thought it over and completed my *SOAP Notes*, and I realized that that informal assessment gave me absolutely no useful information. What if they underlined five words, but none of them were adjectives? I realized, as I did on several other occasions, that I had let the class go without having any real idea of what they knew and didn't know.

The next day I assigned a different type of assessment. The students read three sentences, then identified the adjectives on a small sheet of paper that I collected. After seeing these responses, I had much more useful information about how they were doing and what they needed. *SOAP Notes* reflection helped me become aware of my own errors and correct them the next day. While everyone wishes they could do things perfectly the first time, *SOAP Notes* reflective writing acknowledges that missteps are inevitable. *SOAP Notes* reflective practice allows teachers to learn from and correct their mistakes as they grow alongside their students.

Insight 4: Students' Emotional Needs and Reactions

Finally, one of the most significant areas of insight I discovered during this *SOAP Notes* project was the importance of students' emotional responses to academic tasks, especially related to self-efficacy. As the lessons grew harder and harder, the students responded in a variety of ways. Some students seemed to shut down and disengage, while others grew frustrated. Some expressed to me that they were "just not good at grammar," and no matter how hard they tried, it didn't make sense to them.

These observations I recorded in my *SOAP Notes* reminded me of Vygotsky's (1978) concept of the Zone of Proximal Development where his theory sheds some light on the students' reactions. Vygotsky (1978) noted that there are some tasks students can do easily without help, and some they can do but need support from what he calls "a more knowledgeable other." Finally, beyond these first two levels, there is a range of frustration. For various reasons, related to knowledge level, prior-knowledge preparation, or sometimes even cognitive readiness, students cannot spend much time in this level without becoming overwhelmed and experiencing a high level of failure. Although I was familiar with this theory, my *SOAP Notes* reflections allowed me to see exactly what this looks like in the classroom, how it affects students, and what I can do to make their learning experiences less frustrating and more empowering. As I reflected on these observations, I began to make small changes with the goal that, no matter where they were in their understanding, each student would have the opportunity to experience success at least occasionally during the class period.

One change I made because of my *SOAP Notes* reflections was the simple but effective strategy of rearranging the sentences we studied in a more logical order. I began activities with sentences I knew were far below what the students should be doing at this point. These sentences gave students a chance to review what they already knew, and they boosted their confidence in preparation for what came next. After these initial easy sentences, I designed the order of the sentences that followed so that new concepts were added one at a time. For example, we would begin a diagramming practice with a sentence like, "I drove." The next sentence might say, "I drove quickly," then "I drove quickly to Atlanta."

Later, after writing additional *SOAP Notes* reflections, I began plateauing the sentences rather than making each one more difficult. I would include a few similar-level sentences in a row so that even if students didn't get it on the first try, they had another chance to do a similar exercise. This allowed them to experience redemption and helped them stay encouraged about their own ability to learn. During these types of scaffolding activities, I could see the students improving before my eyes as I helped them less and less. By the end of our practice time, many expressed that they felt much more confident. My *SOAP Notes* reflections helped me to be more aware of my students' emotional responses to the content, find ways to manage their frustration, and give them opportunities to shine.

Limitations

In the interest of presenting a complete portrait of my experiences with reflective practice, I will conclude this chapter with some limitations before sharing my overall thoughts on the experience. There were two potential shortcomings I noticed while engaging in reflective practice. The first was that though reflection was useful for helping me identify problems, it didn't always provide a clear path forward to solve them. I knew that some of my students needed an additional challenge, but I found that even though I was aware of this, I wasn't always knowledgeable about the best ways to extend the content for those who were ready for it.

Reflective writing is most useful not as a stand-alone technique but when used in conjunction with other types of professional development, reading, and observing other teachers. The second potential downfall of *SOAP Notes* reflective practice is that it can lose its effectiveness if it slips into quick assumptions and careless explanations rather than true analysis of a situation. Sometimes when I was confused about why a student had given a particular answer, I attributed it to blind guessing. While this may have occasionally been the case, I found myself writing that more often than any other explanation. It took two levels of reflection—one the day of the lesson and another when I was examining my notes overall—to realize that I was over-using that simple explanation and most likely misunderstanding the situation. *SOAP Notes* reflection can be a useful tool, but I found that its usefulness is also directly related to the effort that is put into it.

Overall Impact and Final Thoughts

As I thought about how daily reflection impacted my instruction, I was hoping for an exciting success story about how student test scores soared in immediate response to the changes I was making each day. The truth is, they didn't. The grades students earned during the time I completed this project were comparable to what they were in earlier units. However, I might still count this as a success because the content was more difficult than what they had encountered in the past. I think what was more significant than test scores were the other, less quantifiable impacts it had on the students and our classroom.

SOAP Notes reflective practice had a positive impact on the relationship I was having with my students. When I adjusted the pace of a unit to allow for more time to practice or came back the next day with a better way to teach something students had struggled with, they noticed. *SOAP Notes* reflective practice, if nothing else, is a simple way to show genuine care for students, and that makes a difference.

A second impact of *SOAP Notes* reflective practice for me was a change in my own perception of my role as a teacher. As I thought about the students, navigating a time when school in general is becoming more difficult and demanding, I realized that facing difficulties and the unknown is not just a part of education, it *is* education. The essence of all education is moving from what you know and are comfortable with to what you don't know and are not sure you can do. Because of this, education will always be an inherently scary and unsettling experience.

My *SOAP Notes* reflections helped me to understand the role I played in this process. Although I can't (and shouldn't) take away all the natural discomfort of learning and growing, I can support students by encouraging them, designing lessons that systematically foster self-efficacy, and simply giving them the time they need to learn and practice. Teachers play a role in building students' confidence and feelings of competency as learners, and *SOAP Notes* reflection can help them to accomplish this important task with thought, care, and empathy.

From the very first day I began this project, writing *SOAP Notes* reflections had an incredibly positive impact on my instruction, despite the few shortcomings of the practice. *SOAP Notes* are a simple yet almost startlingly effective tool for self-assessment, analysis, brainstorming, and strategic planning. If my experiences are any indication, *SOAP Notes* reflection has the potential to be a powerful tool for creating impact in the classroom.

TAKE-AWAYS

SOAP Notes **reflective practice helped:**

- Create self-efficacy and confidence
- Foster student success
- Encourage the creation of actively engaging lessons
- Assess student growth and learning
- Build student–teacher relationships
- Provide more time for teacher mentoring and guiding of student learning

References

Davis, H. (2012). *An interpersonal approach to classroom management* (pp. 23–24). Corwin.

Vygotsky, L. S. (1978). *Mind in society: The development of higher psychological processes*. Harvard University Press.

16

Why Reflective Practice Matters in the Classroom

Jessica Gruesbeck

GETTING TO KNOW THE AUTHOR

- ◆ High school English
- ◆ 4th year of teaching
- ◆ Public charter school
- ◆ Urban setting

While I was completing my *SOAP Notes*, my juniors were reading *The Crucible* and learning about text development and author's choices. Throughout the course of my *SOAP Notes*, students read acts three and four of the play and started their summative assessment, where they had to choose one of the four prompts given to them and write a four- to six-page literary analysis.

Due to the COVID-19 pandemic, this school year is the first "normal" school year many of my students have had. For example, the juniors on whom I took my *SOAP Notes* have not had a normal school year since they were in the eighth grade. I think it is very important for me to note that I have known my juniors,

DOI: 10.4324/9781003493464-25

for the most part, since they were in eighth grade. I became their English teacher when they were sophomores. At the beginning of every school year, and multiple times throughout the year, our students complete the STAR reading test so teachers know their current reading levels. At the beginning of this year, I was astonished by how many students were far, far behind. These were juniors, and some were reading at only a fifth grade level! My heart broke for them.

My students know that I have very high expectations, and therefore expect them to do their work, no matter what. I do accept late work because I believe in forgiveness and second chances, but I push them hard every single day. Through using reflective practice in my classroom, I am able to meet students where they are while also pushing them forward and helping them strive. I know that I've always used reflective practice in my classroom, but it wasn't until I started taking *SOAP Notes* that I realized much of what they do: their body language, their questions, and the discussions we have in class. This helps me decide where to go next in my lessons.

Initially, when we would read an entire play, we would complete a summative assessment and then watch the movie as a reward. However, through SOAP noting, I quickly noticed that this method was not benefiting my students. For example, on the first two days of my *SOAP Notes*, my students were finishing up ACT III of *The Crucible*. Now, anyone who has read *The Crucible* knows that Act III is where the play reaches its climax. So, when I watched my students as they were reading, they were extremely attentive. They all wanted to read aloud, they were all sitting up very straight, paying attention, and contributing to the classroom discussion on the text. They were excited about what they were learning and were really understanding the content.

The next day, day 3, was not so great. One of my district's priority standards has to deal with informational text. This is because our state testing scores tell us that the students do not do well with picking out the main ideas of informational text. Therefore, in my classroom, I incorporate informational text throughout all of my units. The way I do this with *The Crucible* is by using a website called commonlit.org. This is a very great tool to use; teachers can search for different texts, and the website pulls up informational text for the students to read. It also suggests pairing the informational text pieces with the text being taught; sometimes it may be before the text, after the text, or even after specific acts or scenes.

Based on what I recorded in my *SOAP Notes*, while my students were completing their work on day 3, they were very resistant. There were quite a few of them who put their heads down and went to sleep or even just sat on their phones. I wanted the students to complete the assignment by themselves, especially since the questions they see after the reading are very much like the questions they will see on a state test, so I tried my best not to intervene. It bothered me that my students were noncompliant that day. At the end of class, I talked to them about it. I asked them, "Why weren't you doing your work? You've been so good in my class with getting your work done, what changed today?" Their responses astounded me. So many of them told me that they just didn't understand the text. They started to read it, and they couldn't comprehend what it was saying.

I learned through the use of my *SOAP Notes* reflection, when I planned to use informational text in my classroom again, I would try a different approach such as reading it to them. We read it aloud as a class, and I could see that they understood a lot more. They were also more willing to ask questions about the text, which helped them in their comprehension. This speaks volumes to how important reflective practice is within the classroom.

On day 4 of my *SOAP Notes*, the students were back to their normal, excited-to-learn selves. This was because we were starting the last act of *The Crucible*; they were excited to see how it was all going to end. Since we read plays aloud in class, and this act had a lot of characters, I had multiple students so excited that they volunteered to read extra parts without hesitation. They were all sitting up straight, paying very close attention to the reading, and even contributing to class discussion about the happenings of the play.

As stated previously, my students undergo a lot of benchmark (STAR) testing throughout the school year. Therefore, day 6 of my *SOAP Notes* is an outlier. On day 6, my students had to take their second round of benchmark testing. The students are often aware that they struggle with reading, especially at the grade level I teach. When they came into my classroom that day, they were very upset that they had to do testing. I explained to them that I understood their frustration, but that if they just tried their best, that was all that mattered. They did so, and the next day, we finished the movie.

According to my *SOAP Notes*, the students were absolutely enthralled with the ending of the movie and text. They were upset that Proctor allowed himself to die for a crime he did not commit, and they argued very loudly about it in class. Once I got them settled, they had to complete some more questions on the reading, and they performed very well.

Writing is something that my students have always been resistant toward. They don't think they can write well, which is false, for the most part. They just lack confidence, and they get really scared when they're told they have a big writing assignment due. Since I know this from teaching the same kids for at least a year, I know that I would need to give my students plenty of time to work on their essays for this unit—two whole weeks to be exact. I also know that they struggle writing paragraphs that are longer than three to five sentences; therefore I knew exactly how I was going to introduce this essay to them.

The first thing I wrote on day 8 of my *SOAP Notes* was about summative assessment that was an essay assignment. This assessment included the standards covered, the objectives, what they needed to do, what prompts they could choose from, how many points the essay was worth, and a prewriting section. Once the students all had this, I went over it in great detail. When I got to the point that said their essays had to be four to five pages, they froze. The fear in some of their eyes was very real. So I asked them why this seemed so scary to them. I explained that their paragraphs should be 10–11 sentences, and that as long as they did that, they would be okay. Their eyes just about bugged out of their head. So, I stopped right there and went over, in great detail, how to write an argumentative essay.

When teaching students how to write an argumentative essay, I've learned through my *SOAP Notes* reflective practice that the best way to teach them is by using a topic many can agree on: dogs. A lot of people love dogs. I tell them to pretend they're writing an argumentative essay about why dogs are the best pets to have. Then, they came up with three reasons why. Once they did that, I explained to them that those are their claims for the paper. Then, I took one claim, and taught them how to find evidence to support that claim. By using this method, not only have I taught the students how to write longer paragraphs (I make them use a minimum of three pieces of evidence to support each claim), but also, I've taught them how to defend their opinions with textual evidence. This makes the writing process much easier for them. In my *SOAP Notes*, I recorded that they were able to verbally repeat what I taught them, and as they started writing their analysis of *The Crucible*, I realized they were using the correct method.

On days 9 and 10 of my *SOAP Notes*, I noticed that my students were very actively working on their essays. I also noticed, however, that some of them were having a hard time concentrating in the silence for that long. The next day, I had a few of the students ask if I would play music for them to help them concentrate better. I made sure this was okay with the majority of the class, which it was, so I put on some school appropriate music. It helped them focus much better. Because of this day, I have learned to offer to play music for students while they are working silently on essays. Using the *SOAP Notes* to guide me, on day 12, their last day to work on their essay in class, I played music again, and most of my students finished their essays and did very well.

On day 13 and 14 of my *SOAP Notes*, it was time for us to start a new unit. The unit we were starting was all about legal documents. The students were going to read the Declaration of Independence and the Bill of Rights. According to my *SOAP Notes*, my students were extremely unengaged and lacked enthusiasm. They were not into it at all. They didn't understand why they had to read it since the documents were "so old." So my first thought was to teach them why it was important for them to know. Now, as I reflect on that lesson, I know that in the future, I want to make the lesson more fun, so the students are more engaged. One idea is something an old coworker used to do; she would play the Jimmi Hendrix version of the *Star Spangled Banner*.

On day 15, the final day of *SOAP Notes*, my students read the *Bill of Rights*. Before we started reading, I asked the students why it was important for them to know this information, to which they replied that it is their basic rights. Because of them knowing this, they were much more interested in the reading. We read the rights aloud as a class and had a discussion about each one. We also gave examples of situations where those rights would protect us. This is a unit that I will always teach when I have juniors, because it is so vital that they know and understand their rights as citizens in this country, especially in today's society.

Reflective practice is one of the most important parts of being a teacher. You have to be able to look back at what you've taught and how you've taught it and decide if it went well or if you need to change your delivery. Through the use of *SOAP Notes* reflective practice, I noticed that the way I taught something did not always go well with the students, and therefore I needed to modify it so that my students could succeed. That is completely okay. As a teacher, it is our job to make sure that each and every student in our classrooms can learn to the best of their ability. Reflective practice is essential for every teacher to utilize in their classrooms.

TAKE-AWAYS

SOAP Notes **reflective practice helped:**

♦ Revise instructional strategies
♦ Engage students and promote enthusiasm
♦ Identify the teacher delivery system and effectiveness
♦ Analysis of aligning planning and instructional practice

17

Small Pieces, Big Picture

Shoupra Shikwana

GETTING TO KNOW THE AUTHOR

- 7th grade English teacher
- 6th year of teaching
- Suburban middle school

As I sit at my desk at school and reflect on my career as a teacher, I have thought of many ways to share my reflections and the impact of my instruction. Thanks to my middle schoolers who left an unfinished puzzle at the front of the room, I have realized that teaching is like a puzzle. There are hundreds of unique pieces that are different sizes, shapes, and colors. While some pieces may resemble others, each piece is unique, with its own intricate design. As you begin the puzzle, you have a reference photo to look at, but to complete the big picture, you have to match up the small colorful pieces. Using the *SOAP Notes* reflective strategy has helped me complete the puzzle.

Solving the puzzle is just like teaching, especially as a newer teacher. I have references from curriculum maps, mentor or veteran teachers, the state standards, textbooks, and maybe even experience from the previous school year. Each school year is

DOI: 10.4324/9781003493464-26

unique because both the students and I have changed over time. Plus, I have a little more experience under my belt as each year passes. Maybe this year, I will complete the puzzle by finding and matching all of the edge pieces to complete the border first, or I might try something new and attempt to match the puzzle pieces by color, texture, or shape. Will the hooks and knobs of the pieces line up? For me, *SOAP Notes* was the key to fit the pieces together—it bridged the gaps between teaching and learning. Eventually, with time in reflection, I realized what instructional strategies needed to be modified and implemented to ensure student success.

This is the beauty of teaching. There are so many different ways to teach a unit or lesson, but it is up to the teacher to determine the best strategy to take. By using the various sections of *SOAP Notes*, I was able to see the elements of the lesson come together. Through reflective practice, I could evaluate the lesson and decide if I could use it as a roadmap for future lessons. The more experience I have with *SOAP Notes* reflective practice, the easier it will become.

⁎ *⁎* *⁎*

I'll be honest—the beginning of this school year was tough. I genuinely struggled with my classroom management, especially with keeping my students' behaviors in check. This was evident when I reviewed my *SOAP Notes*. My group of students this year were highly social with one another and active in the classroom. They preferred taking their shoes off, putting their legs up, sitting on the floor, or roaming around the room. In addition, they didn't complete their work in a timely manner, and if work was turned in, it tended to be completed without full effort. They wanted to play computer games any chance they had, and they were not interested in learning unless the lesson included their Chromebooks. As I reflected on my *SOAP Notes*, I noticed a consistent pattern and had to remind myself that we needed some time to adjust and work on our routines and behaviors.

Within the *SOAP Notes* template, classroom behaviors were noted in the Subjective, Observation, and Challenge sections (see Table 17.1).

TABLE 17.1 *SOAP Notes:* "Duffy's Jacket"/Elements of Literature Day 1

Evaluation of Instruction (SOAP)	By:	Shoupra Shikwana	Date:	Day 1

S	**Subjective**: students' willingness to participate, demeanor, body language, attitude. Teacher's perceptions and reflections

- ◆ Class began groaning when I told them to open up their textbooks.
  - ◆ "Can I go to the office to get ice? My ankle is suddenly hurting."—A. Reyes
- ◆ A lot of talking before getting started with the lesson
  - ◆ Some students are waiting quietly with textbook open.
  - ◆ R. Ferguson is working on his essay from the last unit. When he was asked to close his CB, he said he only has one paragraph left to finish it.
- ◆ Set expectations for the students before we start listening to the audio. All students are following along with the audio (flipping page at the right time).
  - ◆ Many laughed near the end of the story, "You forgot your jacket, stupid!"
- ◆ S. Davis walked in late @ 8:12 AM.
- ◆ At the end of the story, students take a while to quiet down and struggle with transitions between different activities.
  - ◆ I quietly wait for them to stop talking, and students tell each other to quiet down.
- ◆ Story Questions
  - ◆ I read the questions and explain them, then they answer them on the paper.
  - ◆ All students are working.
  - ◆ Four students volunteer to share answers.
  - ◆ S. Davis is not working.
  - ◆ Give students 30 seconds to share their answer with someone sitting near them.

O	**Observation** of student learning: anecdotal notes

- ◆ Intro to the plot map unit (a review for some students and new for others—depending on the team they were on last year).
- ◆ Students were not happy about having to read a story together, but once the story finished they mentioned how they enjoyed reading / listening to it. They said it reminds them of Mr. Altman and his "dad joke" stories (our science teacher on the team).
- ◆ Many students laughed at the funny parts and were engaged while reading.
- ◆ I could control the story we read in class and can change their minds about reading—might take some time to fully convince them.

(Continued)

TABLE 17.1 (Continued)

Evaluation of Instruction (SOAP)	By:	Shoupra Shikwana	Date:	Day 1
<u>A</u>	**Assessing** student learning: progress monitoring, running records, oral or written comprehension			

- ◆ Students are able to answer setting and characterization questions without rereading the story.
- ◆ Will know more tomorrow after question doc is turned in.
- ◆ Exit ticket
- ◆ Rate "Duffy's Jacket"
  - ◆ ⅘ stars = 60%, ⅗ stars = 26%, 5/5 stars = 13%
- ◆ What lesson did Duffy learn?
  - ◆ 13% said idk, 80% had the correct answer, 7% answered incorrectly.

<u>P</u>	**Planning** for next lesson: use bullet points

- ◆ Will finish the rest of the elements of literature questions tomorrow.
- ◆ We will reread the story one more time before working again.

Challenges: What challenges did you encounter while working with your students?

- ◆ Students staying quiet—a very talkative and social group.

Further Learning: What else do you need to know how to do?

- ◆ Continue working through the elements of literature.
- ◆ Discussing each part and identifying where they are in "Duffy's Jacket" and other short stories.

Source: Weaver, J. C., Hartzog, M., Murnen, T., & Bertelsen, C. D. (2019). Bowling Green State University.

As teachers might predict, classroom behaviors impact classroom instruction. The introductory units the 7th grade English/ Language Arts teachers and I originally planned were taking longer to get through because of the behaviors in my classroom. I was desperate to try anything to keep my group quiet and working; it is laughable how many different strategies I tried just to keep my classes quiet, and I did smile when reviewing my *SOAP Notes* because I noted many instructional strategies. My daily reflections include a new strategy almost every class period.

Some may wonder what any of this has to do with reflecting on my instruction, but I have learned the hard way that classroom management plays a huge role in teaching. The days that I struggle with managing my classroom are the days I am struggling to complete the daily lessons on time. I was constantly trying new strategies to get my group of students to engage in the class. I was desperate to find anything that could work.

If we fast forward a few months, I am less frustrated, and we are getting through our planned lessons with ease. While my classroom management is not perfect, I have found a few strategies that have worked for me and my current group of students. Through reflection and trial and error, I have found methods to create a positive learning environment that supports student success. By continuing to implement this positive learning environment, I am able to keep up with the pacing of each unit and stay on track with the other 7th grade ELA classes in the building. Through the use of reflective practice and noting those practices that are successful with my students, I have come to genuinely enjoy spending time with them each day.

Getting to Know Students

I made it a goal to get to know my 7th graders as students and as people. Along with that, I wanted them to get to know me as a teacher and as a person, as well. As teachers it is important to gather necessary information and data about our students to guide our teaching. We can do this before even meeting our students by checking the student cumulative files and gathering reading lexiles, state test scores, and grades in previous grade levels.

One assessment I use to gather data is having students write a brief essay to determine their writing ability at the beginning of the year and ask them to take a survey to determine their learning styles. I ask them to complete pre-assessments, and within the first couple of months, I have a good understanding of their work habits. Through these assessments and further reflection, I began to realize that I did not know much about many of my students.

Based on all pre-assessment data, I started with simple daily ice breaker questions during each class period's attendance. Rather than calling each student's name on my roster and having them respond with "Here," I would ask a get-to-know-you question. I tried to find a balance between serious and silly topics, and I wanted to make sure each student in the room had a voice. The students were excited to find out the question of the day, to share their answers with their peers, and to hear others' responses. As I reflected using *SOAP Notes*, not only did I note a change in classroom behavior, but I also realized it was a refreshing way to engage students and begin each class period (see Table 17.2).

TABLE 17.2 *SOAP Notes:* "Duffy's Jacket"/Elements of Literature Day 2

Evaluation of Instruction (SOAP)	*By:*	Shoupra Shikwana	*Date:*	Day 2
S	**Subjective**: students' willingness to participate, demeanor, body language, attitude. Teacher's perceptions and reflections			

- Started the class with a Quizlet to review Elements of Literature terms (plot map, exposition, climax, etc.), and students were excited to play LIVE!
  - "Is this like a pre-test?"—C. Battles
  - A few students were frustrated with the new terms (M. Koback was visibly angry), and the Quizlet Live took longer than anticipated.
- Rereading the story for a second time—three students had wandering eyes and needed redirections.
  - The class still laughed at the same funny parts from yesterday.
- Students worked in groups of three to complete the elements of literature questions and were only allowed to ask me two questions per group—I told them I was collecting and grading the packets.
  - Most groups were on task and completed their work.
  - Two questions per group was awesome—they asked each other their questions before having to ask me—used their resources.
- 4/5 groups completed their assignment; one group did not—they were stuck on question 1 for a majority of the class period – they needed many reminders to move on, but they could not agree on their answers.
  - "The narrator reminds me of Lemony Snicket" M. Koback "The narrator doesn't remind me of Lemony Snicket … explain what you meant"—C. Butungi

(Continued)

TABLE 17.2 (Continued)

O	**Observation** of student learning: anecdotal notes
	◆ After explaining the importance of rereading stories, the students did not mind reading the story again. ◆ The students enjoyed working in small groups—it allowed them to be social in a productive way in order to complete their assignment.
A	**Assessing** student learning: progress monitoring, running records, oral or written comprehension
	◆ Setting: 5/5 groups answered this section correctly ◆ Characterization: 3/5 groups completed this section correctly; 2/5 groups did not complete: 1/5 did not attempt and 1/5 only attempted the extended response about the importance of connecting to characters ◆ Conflict: 5/5 groups answered this question correctly ◆ Rising action: 2/5 groups answered this portion correctly; 3/5 either not complete or not correct ◆ Climax: only one group answered this correctly ◆ Resolution: 3/5 correct; 2/5 not attempted
P	**Planning** for next lesson: use bullet points
	◆ Next week we will discuss the answers to this assignment and move on to the next story, "Rikki Tikki Tavi"; based on the results of this assignment the students need most focus on the climax of the story. This story will touch on all parts of the elements of literature unit, but I can spend more time on the climax of the story when we start to read it.
Challenges: What challenges did you encounter while working with your students?	
	◆ There were not many challenges while the students were working. All of the groups were working quietly with the goal of completing their work. Only one group had a difficult time agreeing on their answers before moving on. Some groups divided and conquered, while others focused on one question at a time.
Further Learning: What else do you need to know how to do?	
	◆ I would like to keep using small groups for assignments in the future—I may have to change up the groups to split up the one that did not complete as much work as the rest of the groups.

Unfortunately, these quick and easy icebreaker questions were not the golden answer I was looking for. During our Elements of Literature unit in October and November, I struggled with many students in my first period class, but Mary is one student whom I wish I approached differently. Even though it was a few months into the school year, I already started getting to know a majority of my students. Mary was a newer student in our building and I still had a lot to learn about her. After looking through my notes, she is mentioned 11 times within 15 class periods. Sixty-three percent of the time that Mary was mentioned was because of a challenge she was creating for me in my classroom. I used the *SOAP Notes* to record some individual student behavior and how I would address it in the next class or later that day (see Table 17.3).

Because of my reflection and my attention to overcome the challenges Mary presented in class, I was able to intentionally

TABLE 17.3 *SOAP Notes:* "Duffy's Jacket"/Elements of Literature Day 3

Evaluation of Instruction (SOAP)	By:	Shoupra Shikwana	Date:	Day 3
S	**Subjective**: students' willingness to participate, demeanor, body language, attitude. Teacher's perceptions and reflections			

- ◆ Started class with context clues warm-up (essential vocab in "Rikki Tikki Tavi")—I originally gave time to work on it independently, but many students just sat there doing nothing / I walked them through how to do complete the assignment with the first word (define using a context clue, three synonyms, use the word in a sentence). Students completed rest on their own.
  - ◆ "I like doing these. Can we do them more often?"—A. Reyes
  - ◆ Six students volunteered to participate when reviewing words.
- ◆ When the independent reading slide popped up on the screen, everyone quickly and quietly took out their independent reading novel and reading logs.
  - ◆ "Yay! I miss reading"—K. DeMoss
  - ◆ All students were quietly reading for 15 minutes.
- ◆ Students were quiet while reviewing answers for the "Duffy's Jacket" elements of plot questions.
- ◆ Students were eager when watching the King Cobra video to preview "Rikki Tikki" and for the internet scavenger hunt for the mongoose, king cobra, and bungalow

(Continued)

TABLE 17.3 (Continued)

_O_	**Observation** of student learning: anecdotal notes
	◆ Students seemed interested while watching the king cobra video. ◆ They enjoyed making their own sentences with the new vocabulary words. ◆ They liked the internet scavenger hunt, and all successfully completed that assignment. ◆ A few students were zoned out through a majority of the class period (S. Davis, J. Moseley, M. Watkins).
_A_	**Assessing** student learning: progress monitoring, running records, oral or written comprehension
	◆ Students were assessed when we discussed the answers to the vocab doc—students volunteered to answer(formative assessment) — maybe I should have pulled name cards instead to widen the range of student participation? ◆ Will be useful for future context clues assignments. ◆ Students successfully found information on the mongoose, king cobra, and bungalow.
_P_	**Planning** for next lesson: use bullet points
	◆ Will do the same activity with the next set of vocabulary words from the story. ◆ Quizlet to review the new words before reading the story? ◆ Set the scene before reading (main characters are mongoose and king cobra, and setting = bungalow).
Challenges: What challenges did you encounter while working with your students?	
	◆ Challenge with starting the warm-up; had to walk the students through the activity. ◆ No other challenges. ◆ Struggling with smooth transitions in between activities assignments.
Further Learning: What else do you need to know how to do?	
	◆ We will continue practicing the warm-up that we had today with context clues. Three new vocabulary words that will be found in the "Rikki Tikki Tavi" short story.

address my interactions with her to ensure and support her success. After many uncomfortable, awkward, and sometimes frustrating moments in class, Mary and I were able to improve our relationship. I tried to be more supportive of her and her learning, and she tried extra hard on assignments and participated more in class. Mary moved away soon after we finally repaired our relationship, but she surprised me by sending me an email expressing how much she missed me and that she designed a new mask for me that said, "Best English teacher ever!" It was a bittersweet moment to receive such a sweet email from her.

As a result of further reflection, I have made it a goal to give my students room to speak when I don't understand where they are coming from and to try to understand their point of view. I try to create an open dialogue. I do think these one-on-one moments of dialogue give the students an opportunity to respect me more as a person and teacher. Once we have our conversations and understand each other, the classroom environment is more positive.

Positive Incentives

While taking the time to get to know my students on a personal level, I was still trying to find ways to improve my classroom management and instruction on a bigger level. Now that I know my students a little better, I tried to think of ways to motivate my 7th graders. I began to brainstorm and reflect on positive incentives for my students to work toward.

In my *SOAP Notes*, I noted the incorporation of various incentives I used as assessments—for example, Books Bingo lottery boards, Kahoot, class raffles, marble jars, and other live interactive class games. There have been times where I have connected Books Bingo to our positive behavior incentive system (PBIS) word of the month.

The Books Bingo lottery boards include 25 blank spaces for students to sign if they contribute to class in a positive way. This can include but is not limited to participating often, being a leader, or providing a profound answer during a discussion.

Once the boards are filled up, we have a class raffle with five winners. Reflecting in my *SOAP Notes*, I was beginning to notice that the Books Bingo boards were not enough for my current group of students. I was beginning to realize that some students were earning spots on the board far more often than the others, and I needed a class reward system that would motivate all students in the room. I asked some of the experienced staff members I work with for advice. My RESA mentor introduced me to the idea of having marble jars in class along with the bingo boards. Marble jars is a whole class reward system. If the class is following expectations, they will earn marbles to fill up their jar, and once the class jar is filled, the whole class gets a prize.

These classroom reward systems have been life changing. This has been a great way to motivate all of the students in the room to work and stay on task during the class period. It also helped with classroom management. Since incorporating both systems in our daily routine, we complete our lessons in a timely manner. These reward systems give the students small and achievable goals to work toward, and they are able to hold one another accountable for their actions. Not to mention that these class rewards also allow all of us to have something fun to look forward to each week.

Piecing It All Together

These components that I have mentioned may not seem significant, but they have changed the way I approach teaching and the impact reflection has on student learning, engagement, and classroom management. I am always looking for ways to improve what I do, but I am confident that these small pieces impact the bigger picture. I am able to personalize my lessons each day to the experiences of the students sitting in my classroom. Creating small and achievable goals for my students to work toward together creates a positive learning environment for everybody in the room.

I am hopeful that this year's puzzle will be framed as a reference for next year. Keeping track of what has worked for me through *SOAP* Noting will help me have a head start when I meet my next group of students next year. If you find yourself struggling with your classes, remember that "even the hardest puzzles have a solution."

TAKE-AWAYS

SOAP Notes **reflective practice helped:**

♦ Engage students
♦ Maintain positive classroom management
♦ Deepen student and teacher relationships
♦ Identify innovative classroom management strategies

Part IV

Conclusion

18

Teacher Voices

Final Wrap-Up

Joanna C. Weaver and Cynthia D. Bertelsen

GETTING TO KNOW THE AUTHORS

♦ Joanna C. Weaver, Ph.D. is an associate professor
  ♦ Adolescence to young adult integrated language arts
  ♦ Graduate reading
  ♦ Bowling Green State University
♦ Cynthia D. Bertelsen, Ph.D. is an associate professor emeritus
  ♦ Early childhood education
  ♦ Graduate reading
  ♦ Bowling Green State University

The authors of our chapters had revelations about their practice that were unexpected and discovered that *SOAP Notes* could be used for several purposes. For example, Amy (Chapter 11) found that the use of *SOAP Notes* elevated student voices when she encouraged her students to use the *SOAP Notes* template to

DOI: 10.4324/9781003493464-28

record the impact of nonverbal behaviors. In addition, teachers discovered more about themselves as facilitators beyond the learning needs of their students.

As facilitators of this project, we were curious how teachers would utilize *SOAP Notes* in their classrooms and the impact this type of reflective practice had on their instructional decision-making and student growth. Our own queries led us to ask teachers: How did they apply the use of *SOAP Notes* in their classrooms? and How did recording *SOAP Notes* impact their teaching practices and student learning? Using these questions, we could definitely see some similarities when the teachers discussed the benefits of *SOAP Notes* and student growth. These similarities and differences are noted in Table 18.1. We have identified below several benefits and impacts on student learning that the teachers noted.

Benefits of *SOAP Notes*

Reading the chapters, teachers reflected on the impact of *SOAP Notes* and delineated the benefits of reflective practice on their instructional decision-making. For example, Erin (Chapter 9) noted, "Looking retrospectively at my notes, I was able to see growth in my own teaching and mental health." Emily (Chapter 6) emphasized this as well when she stated, "*SOAP Notes* helps teachers to pay attention to not only the 'education' side of their job, but also the *human* side." In addition, Amy (Chapter 11) stated, "Sometimes [*SOAP Notes*] confounded and challenged me, which created the most growth for me because it called on me to discover, then plan, and act on what I needed to know as educator."

Several teachers noted in their chapters other instructional benefits. For instance, Anna (Chapter 8) stated, "[it] helped me to make more positive changes in my classroom" and Julianna (Chapter 15) noted, "A second impact of reflective practice for me was a change in my own perception of my role as a teacher." Furthermore, Matt (Chapter 3) reported the importance of the written documentation, stating, "Many of these subjective thoughts are often lost from year to year when we reteach a lesson because educators simply do not remember all the little details of how the students reacted to the content."

Impact on Student Growth

As teachers reflected using *SOAP Notes*, they reflected on student learning and became more aware of the formative and summative assessments that best reflected student growth. For example, Allison (Chapter 4) stated,

> With *SOAP Notes*, that same teacher can have the opportunity to really identify how students interacted with the lesson, what went wrong, how it went wrong, and what they can do to revise the lesson to be able to try again (Pamer, Chapter 3).

Furthermore, Gabrielle (Chapter 5) discussed how she was able to reflect on her instructional challenges with collaborative group work and online teaching.

> These notes are indicative of an overall sense I had that students were not getting as much out of these lessons as they could be, leaving me to wonder how I could use these takeaways to help improve my instruction in a way that will get students to participate more.

SOAP Notes enabled teachers to identify student interests that guided their instruction. Lizzi (Chapter 14) noted, "I hope to continue using reflective practices in my lesson planning in order to help my students find their passions, find success, and find a love for learning." In addition, Julianna (Chapter 15) stated, "My reflections helped me to be more aware of my students' emotional responses to the content, find ways to manage their frustration, and give them opportunities to shine."

TABLE 18.1 Topic Reflective Takeaways

	Chapter 1	Chapter 2	Chapter 3	Chapter 4	Chapter 5	Chapter 6	Chapter 7	Chapter 8
Takeaways	*Pharm D*	*9th grade*	*9th grade*	*HS*	*8th grade*	*HS & CCP*	*HS*	*MS*
A more student-centered classroom							X	
Accurately organizes patient records	X							
Analysis of aligning planning and instructional practice								
Ask critical questions for instructional effectiveness			X					
Assess student growth and learning								
Build and strengthen writing strategies								
Build confidence in instructional decision-making								
Build instructional confidence								
Build student confidence and success								
Build student-teacher relationships								
Confirm non-verbal student responses								

Chapter 9	Chapter 10	Chapter 11	Chapter 12	Chapter 13	Chapter 14	Chapter 15	Chapter 16	Chapter 17
MS	MS	HS	Elementary	8th grade	MS	MS	HS	7th grade
							X	
						X		
					X			
			X					
	X							
					X			
						X		
		X						

(*Continued*)

TABLE 18.1 (Continued)

	Chapter 1	Chapter 2	Chapter 3	Chapter 4	Chapter 5	Chapter 6	Chapter 7	Chapter 8
Takeaways	Pharm D	9th grade	9th grade	HS	8th grade	HS & CCP	HS	MS
Construct strategies for student success								
Create intentionality in passage selection								
Create self-efficacy and confidence								
Deepen student and teacher relationships								
Design and reflect on curriculum								
Develop active student participation							X	
Elevate student learning through critical thinking								
Elevate student successes								
Encourage the creation of actively engaging lessons								
Engage students								
Engage students and promote enthusiasm								
Enhance class culture								
Establish goals	X							

Chapter 9	Chapter 10	Chapter 11	Chapter 12	Chapter 13	Chapter 14	Chapter 15	Chapter 16	Chapter 17
MS	MS	HS	Elementary	8th grade	MS	MS	HS	7th grade
	X							
			X					
						X		
								X
	X							
	X							
X								
						X		
								X
							X	
		X						

Conclusion

> Reflective practice is one of the most important parts of being a teacher. You have to be able to look back at what you've taught and how you've taught it and decide if it went well or if you need to change your delivery.
>
> (Gruesback, Chapter 16)

While reading the chapters, we realized that many of the teachers agreed with Jessica and her perception of reflective practice. They realized the power of reflective practice. Gabrielle (Chapter 5) stated, "Working through the process of engaging in reflective practice has absolutely impacted my students, classroom, and instruction in a positive way. I am able to better accommodate my students' needs."

The chapters within this book elevate teacher voices as they reflect on the powerful impact of their *SOAP Notes* experiences. *SOAP Notes* reflective practice prepares educators to articulate the strengths and weaknesses within their instructional decision-making. It promotes revision based on student engagement and motivation. Reflective practice is a journey that continues over time to empower teachers to embrace reflection focused on instruction and student growth.

For Product Safety Concerns and Information please contact our
EU representative GPSR@taylorandfrancis.com Taylor & Francis
Verlag GmbH, Kaufingerstraße 24, 80331 München, Germany